This book is for research purposes only. This book in no way glorifies nor condones the crime of murder. The theories put forward in this work is done so that it offers an alternate view into the psychological mindset of a criminal perpetrator, as a means of prompting further research and understanding.

Empathy in Death

This book is dedicated to my family, Kelly, Saya, my sister Charlene, and my dearly departed mother Lynda. As well as to every person I have had the privilege to discuss my research with.

Empathy in Death

CHAPTERS AND CONTENTS

<u>EMPATHY IN DEATH</u>

<u>An alternate view at remorse in Serial Killers.</u>

The subject of death has always been a fascinating one for many people. Whether it be in the form of popular fiction, historic events, or as with the current trends filling our television screens and latest book releases, with True Crime. Historical subjects have filtered their way through the ages, only to have been reinvented in the form of entertainment programmes and documentaries, all with the same focus. That being the satisfaction of what can only be described as a form of savage blood lust.

An example of such blood lust making its way onto our silver screens would be that of the popular television series "Vikings". This is a show that is steeped in tradition and folklore. People are drawn to the imagery that the ancient Vikings bring to our modern-day interest. While a great deal of the attraction for a program of this nature is indeed the alure of the tales of a civilisation which has been handed down to us as history throughout the ages, the fundamental lure of these stories cannot be ignored. Despite the fascination of revisiting a forgotten kingdom, it is the carnage and destruction that the Viking nation brought to many a European shore that captures our attention. Tales of the brutality of their plunders, the barbaric styles of the executions and the merciless killing that this once great nation brought, is probably of the greatest factors in what makes the interest in them so fascinating.

Looking back throughout history, it is not only the Viking's carnage which encapsulates our morbid interests. A quick look at the History channels on TV from across the world, there is an almost certainty, that a program about the Second World War is nothing more than a few clicks away on a television remote control. However, a quick summary on what is in fact on offer, shows without question, that there are far more TV documentaries available that show the plight of the Holocaust victims and the atrocities inflicted by the German Nazi forces, as opposed to programs on the British and Allied forces.

Why is that? The popularity of these programmes does not suggest that people are sympathisers with the Nazi cause, in fact quite the contrary. The vast majority of people condemn the actions and atrocities of the Nazi forces and quite rightly so. However, that does not explain as to why programmes pertaining to the death camps and brutality of the Nazi's tends to be a more popular viewing choice.

The reason for that is intrigue. People are drawn to tragedy and brutality as a form of viewing choice out of a sense of fascination and wonder. There seems to be an overwhelming sense of fear and incomprehensibility at the actions of others throughout history, that make being able to turn our attention away from such tragedy, almost impossible to do. There is, in a sense, a possibility of satisfying our own interests of the witnessing of carnage, albeit from the safety of the living room, without having to feel the fear that it might actually "happen to us".

There is a fascination and eternal question that, despite the wish to satisfy our own curiosity, how people in history have been able to act with such brutality, to follow instruction without question or remorse. There has always been a quiet comfort within people who are drawn to these types of topics, that while having an eagerness to learn about these subjects, however, all the while we emotionally distance ourselves from these types of perpetrators. These perpetrators have clearly been identified as "monsters" and while we hold interest in the subject matter, we watch in the comfort that we as the public, do not have the mental capacity to be able to relate to these "monsters" on any level.

The very same can be said of people who engage in the interest of True Crime, more specifically, with Serial Killers. The viewer or reader finds themselves watching or reading the tales of a Serial Killer, all the while distancing themselves from having any form of emotional or mental connection with their personalities, as these Serial Killers are, much in the same way in we view the Nazi's, "Monsters" in our eyes. Thus, giving the viewer or reader the ability to find comfort in continuing their pursuit of interest, all the while knowing that they traditionally, have nothing in common with the "monster" that they are taking the interest in.

What if I told you that this was not the case? It is understandable that a great deal many people would not wish to think that a Serial Killer was anything other than a sub-human species. That the Serial Killer was nothing more than the "Monster" that they had initially perceived them to have been. It has been noted that a Serial Killer is a person who is void of compassion, void of remorse and in some cases, void of the sense that they are doing something that the ordinary person would not.

There are certain indicators that some of these Serial Killers do in fact, display remorse, display grief and even emotion. I will even go as far as to offer up an alternate scenario in which, should there not have been a catalyst for the killer's horrendous actions, then their lives could have turned out completely different. Even as far as the murderous lifestyle potentially being abandoned in its entirety. Naturally, certain psychological factors will have come into connection with the killer's actions, however, there has also been instances in where zero neurological impairment factors have been present. I will of course, cover as much of this basis as possible.

While it may be true that a great deal many of these Serial Killers do not display any forms of remorse, it is my personal belief that this is not always the case. Despite continuously studying psychology, I am not by any means a Psychiatric expert in terms of how the human mind works. However, I have spent a great deal of time speaking to people who have been deemed as Serial Killers, people who have been intimately involved with Serial Killers and in addition, in the absence of my own psychological expertise, I have spoken to professionals trained in the field, as to the plausibility of my theory being sustainable.

This book is in no way being set out to glorify the actions of Serial Killers, quite the contrary. Further to this, I am also not looking to state that my theory is factually proven. I am merely offering out an alternative possibility of thought that my theory could lead to the expansion as to the mindset of people who commit these serial crimes.

In my opinion, the study as to the mindset of Serial Killers is one that, until the eradication of serial murder is complete, then nor shall our studies into why it manifests, be complete either.

This is a journey into a potential alternate world of the mind of a Serial Killer. In a sense, giving a form of "food for thought". I always make the quote that the only darkness that exists, is the one inside of our own imagination. Therefore, it is that darkness that I wish to shed some light on and potentially offer up a new way that we can look at cases such as these.

A Case of Sliding Doors

The Life of Ted Bundy

The theory of Sliding doors is one that emanated in the Twentieth Century, in where a series of inconsequential events at the time would lead to a potential change in the trajectory of future events.

A simple example of such an inconsequential event would be in where a young person who has ideals of beginning studying for a new career, misses their train home after a day's work, because they had stopped for a drink on route to their usual train station. In doing so, when they went to the local store after departing the later train, they go to the book section of the store, perhaps in search of subject matter to discover a subject that may hold study interest. However, just moments prior to this, another person had come along and purchased the last book on the shelf relating to the field of Law, a subject that this person would certainly have been interested in. As there were now no books on the shelf pertaining to Law, the person then notices a book which is about the subject of animal welfare. They pick up this book and as such, purchase it. The person then finds themselves captivated by the subject of caring for animals and in turn, decides to pursue their studies with a view to becoming a veterinarian.

Naturally, it could be said that either of these professions are highly regarded and either would be seen in a positive light for any aspiring career person. However, should it not have been for that decision from the person to stop and have one drink after work, they would not have missed their regular train home on that day and as such, they would have been in the store earlier than the person who actually purchased the book on Law Therefore, they would have most likely have purchased the Law book themselves, with the ideal of becoming a Vet not being in the forefront of their mind.

This is just one example, an example in where the ultimate outcome would be deemed a success. However, there could have been countless other moments in life such as this which could have projected this person's life in a variety of different ways beyond. The decision of a high-profile member of society perhaps bringing in their beloved family pet to his Veterinary practice on a specific day, the opportunity to treat this high-profile person's pet, with the adulation and appreciation from the high-profile person that could have opened up more doors to this Vet in the future. Perhaps even, the high-profile person becoming insistent on this Vet being the sole person to look after all of their pets and animals out of trust. That trust evolving to the point in where the high-profile person wishes this vet to become the sole leader of a rich and prestigious animal welfare society. While this is all merely speculation, none of it could even be remotely possible should the person not have decided to stop for that solitary drink that one day after work.

This is clearly an example in where there was a positive outcome. However, what if we applied this theory to someone like the infamous Serial Killer, Theodore Robert Bundy. What if there was a sliding doors scenario in his life which could have changed the course of his own history?

It has been said on many occasions that Ted Bundy was a killer who murdered his victims (believed to be in the region of thirty-six in total) without any showing any form of remorse or empathy. The killer who has essentially become immortalised in True Crime history as one of the most sadistic and relentless killers of the Twentieth Century. Bundy dispatched his victims without any empathy and did nothing following his capture to provide any form of closure to the families of his victims. However, following his execution of the 24th of January 1989, his brain was dissected during an autopsy, in search of neurological abnormalities, which would give indication as to why he might have killed in the manner in which he did.

Ultimately, there was nothing irregular in Ted Bundy's brain that was able to provide such insight. Instead, all that people were left to rely on when diagnosing Bundy's condition, were a series of behavioural patterns, interviews, and legal reports, as well as information that was taken from speaking to those that knew him prior to his capture and indeed, during the time that he was said to have been actively killing.

The conclusion as to Ted Bundy's diagnosis, according to Al Carlisle PhD, in where the Psychiatric evaluation of Ted Bundy was delivered as being that of an Antisocial Personality Disorder. The characteristics of a person diagnosed with this issue would be displaying factors such as Egocentrism, acting on personal gratification (much in the same that a Psychopath would) an obvious lack of empathy and remorse, an inability to maintain intimate relationships and other factors such as manipulation techniques, coercion, as well as being irresponsible and compulsive (also known traits with psychopaths).

While I am not going to delve too deep into the smaller details of Bundy's murders themselves, there are aspects of that diagnosis that there could potentially be fault with. This is in no way suggesting that the diagnosis given to Ted Bundy was entirely inaccurate, as it goes without question that Ted Bundy was a disturbed person, as would be anyone who committed crimes such as these.

What I do offer up, however, that the blanket diagnosis of merely being an Antisocial Personality Disorder, is perhaps a little too vague to cover the mental condition of such a notorious killer. The reasons being that, while Ted Bundy was egocentric in his viewpoints, he was anything but impulsive in his approach towards his crimes.

Ted Bundy was an intelligent person, that there can be no doubt about. His crimes, however, do not seem to have been undertaken out of sheer impulse. Impulse in itself would mean that the committing of the crimes would have been done without the thought of consequence. Clearly this was not the case with Ted Bundy. Bundy nigh on stalked some of his victims, looked for opportunity, so much so that when the opportunity seemed to retract itself, Bundy was able to grasp a hold of his impulses in order to move onto another victim when the opportunity was guaranteed a higher chance of success without detection. Ted Bundy constructed a rouse, a rouse which made it easier for him to obtain his victims and as such, dispose of their bodies in a manner which would lead to his ultimate detection becoming far more difficult.

Granted that in the latter part of his killing spree, he did become reckless to a degree, acting on impulse in the Chi Omega murders in Florida, after having been foiled in an abduction attempt earlier that evening. There was, however, one major factor in him becoming reckless. Other than the frustration he felt at his earlier, failed exploits, there was the influence of alcohol in his system. Something which has been testified to following his arrest. The effect of alcohol would have most certainly have lowered his inhibitions with regard to controlling his impulses in this situation, therefore in my opinion, lowering his ability to comprehend any form of consequences at the time.

In my book, **Lord of the Dead** in where I wrote the book based on interviews with Nicolas Claux, the Parisian murderer who was dubbed the "Vampire of Paris". Nicolas explains that, while in prison, he noticed the difference between the Psychopath and the Sociopath. He likened the Psychopath as being not dissimilar to that of the mindset of a spoiled child, who would throw a tantrum at the prospect of not being able to get what they wanted at the time, a tantrum which would have been done without the thought of potential consequences as to their actions. Whereas, the Sociopath would be more calculated in their approach, paying close attention to the potential risk involved and therefore, despite eventually acting on their impulses, they would be doing the most that they could to minimise risk to themselves by being caught. It is worth noting, that Nicolas Claux, in addition to being the self-confessed Vampire and Cannibal, as well as convicted murderer, had also studied Psychology in Paris in the 1990's.

Finding variables in the diagnosis that has been placed on Ted Bundy, I cannot help but think that there is a possibility of finding more. While I do think that some of the traits attributed to Ted Bundy are accurate, it remains a possibility to be open to thinking that the diagnosis is still somewhat of a blanket diagnosis, even leaning on vague at times, in where some of the theories have been manoeuvred to fit the profile of Ted

Bundy, as opposed to discovering a new form of diagnosis fitted for Bundy himself.

In Ted Bundy's final interview. A forty-five-minute interview, just hours before his execution, with Rev. Dr James Dobson, Bundy spoke freely and candidly about his life and crimes, in where he placed the emphasis on the events that led to his killings at the hands of violent pornography. I shall come back to the issue of the influence of violent pornography in a short while, however, for the moment I would like to concentrate on Bundy's words with the esteemed Reverend with regards to his victims.

At this point in the proceedings, Ted Bundy had little to gain in terms of saving himself from execution by the electric chair, he understood that his words would have very little effect in terms of changing his ultimate fate. Yet, in this interview, Bundy gave account of what he had done to victims, not in terms of specific detail, but more in the fact that he was sorry for what he had done. He understood that he would not receive forgiveness from the families of the victims, nor that he felt that he would have had any reason as to why he would have deserved such forgiveness. However, he stated that had hoped that the families were able to at least find some peace. Then the topic of discussion came around to that of Kimberly Leach, a twelve-year-old girl that he had abducted, sexually assaulted, and then murdered in 1978. When pressed to discuss this, Bundy could be seen to having struggled to bring himself to speak about what he had done to the young girl. At this stage in proceedings, Bundy had been able to discuss his crimes, even if it was as a means to state his absolution in the eyes of God, yet when it came to the subject of this young girl, Bundy was clearly not able to battle his emotions or demons in order to discuss the young girl.

With the diagnosis of the Antisocial Personality Disorder giving the suggestion that a person of Ted Bundy's ilk, not being able to display empathy or remorse, it could be argued that Bundy's emotion with regards to Kimberly Leach would be a contradiction of this diagnosis. In a statement made by Rev Dr James Dobson, made to the public following his interview with Ted Bundy, the Reverend, who, as well as being a man of the Church, is also in fact a qualified Psychiatrist, the Rev Dr Dobson stated that he felt as though he felt as though Bundy's remorse was genuine. Therefore, in a manner of speaking, going against the blanket diagnosis that had been placed upon Ted Bundy. His professional opinion was that such a man was in fact able to show remorse.

The opening statement in this chapter regarding the sliding door theory is where it now come into place. If the belief in that Ted Bundy was not in control of his emotions and therefore, essentially destined to kill, then there would be little point in trying to see that an alternate scenario was indeed possible. However, given Bundy's words and the statements made by Rev Dr James Dobson in that the emotion displayed by Ted Bundy was genuine, it remains entirely plausible that Ted Bundy was not void of emotion and as such, empathy, and remorse. Giving insight to the fact that his life could have turned out different.

The life of Ted Bundy seemed to take its most dramatic turn, as it seems, by the dissolution of his relationship with Diane Edwards. Edwards was from an affluent family in California and had met Ted Bundy at University in Washington in 1968. Ted Bundy met Edwards while he was studying

Chinese and the two soon began a romantic relationship. As Ted Bundy was working two minimum wage jobs at the time, he had aspirations of the life and esteemed position that the Edwards family seemed to have. Further to this, Ted Bundy had become involved with the Republican Party campaigns and as such, had attended the Party's national conference that same year. Ted Bundy's aspirations towards this lifestyle had essentially led him to having made an emotional connection towards Edwards, even though it could have been said that his emotions were probably more in connection towards the lifestyle that he did not possess, rather than towards Edwards herself.

It was the demise of this relationship that seemed to trigger what would have been what criminal profilers call a "stressor" in terms of Bundy's devolution process towards the start of the ultimate killings. Especially when it can be seen that part of the signature in Ted Bundy's victims were that the victims bore somewhat of a resemblance to Diane Edwards.

In the book by Stephen Michaud and Hugh Aynesworth, ***Ted Bundy: Conversations with a killer***. Ted Bundy discusses his crimes with the two Authors, as though he is speaking in the third person about what a killer "might" have done. Clearly Bundy was speaking about himself, however, as he was still working on a set of appeals, maintaining his innocence as a means to gain his freedom, he did not feel at liberty to incriminate himself further by means of discussing the crimes in the first person.

It can be noted from his conversations with both Michaud and Aynesworth, that the third person that Bundy was speaking of at the time, was more focussed as the crimes being a form of self-gratification. In this,

Bundy explained that the motive for the crimes was not for the purposes of murder. In fact, the sole mindset of the crimes was related to that of sexual assault. It could have been perceived that owing to the similarities in the physical features of both Edwards and that of Bundy's victims, that the sexual assaults could have been deemed as revenge attacks, as a form of a vicarious revenge on Diane Edwards.

In the book, Bundy spoke of the murders as potentially being a means only to silence the sexual assault victims, so that they would not be able to identify the killer at a later time. He concluded that the killings would have been done swiftly, as murder was not the priority, but rather more as a necessity to avoid detection.

That being said, it leaves room for speculation as to what might have happened should his relationship not have broken down with Diane Edwards. It has been said that Edwards thought Bundy to be somewhat childish and immature in nature, which led her to feel disillusioned with their relationship. Therefore, it could be deduced that should Bundy have not displayed these characteristics which would have been seen as a negative trait in the eyes of Edwards, then there could have been hope for their relationship. Therefore, setting about the possibility for a sliding doors theory.

As a bright person, who would have had connections to affluent family circles, as well as the Republican Party, Bundy could have become an affluent person himself. There is no doubt that Bundy was a person who was deemed to having been coercive, therefore, it is entirely possible that Bundy could have used these traits to have made a career for himself in politics. A rise within the Republican Party could have, with the correct set of opportunities and coercive behaviour that wasn't detected by his peers may have even led, over time, to a high-powered position such as a senator for example.

Given that it has been common understanding that sexual scandal has been prevalent in some politicians over the years, should Bundy have felt the need for sexual deviance, there would have been plenty of opportunity and possibility for this. However, given the fact that the "stressor" element would have been taken out of the equation, it is quite plausible that there would not have been the requirement for vicarious revenge on the image of Edwards.

As this potential theory is merely speculative, there is nothing to suggest that the relationship would not have broken down at a later date, however, given that by this time

Bundy may have been in a more affluent position, there would have been more of a risk involved by indulging in things such as murder. The most estimated form of any kind of revenge, would most likely have come from forms of legal battles and litigation.

In summary with regards to Ted Bundy, with or without the potential for a sliding doors scenario, is that Ted Bundy did seem to have an emotional stressor catalyst. That combined with the seemingly genuine remorse for the Kimberly Leach case, gives rise to a belief that whilst not entirely intact, the emotional aspects within the brain of Ted Bundy were present. Despite allowing himself to be swayed by his stressor, or even the violent pornography in his claims, there is a clear indicator that the blanket diagnosis of displaying an Antisocial Personality Disorder, while having traits of accuracy in parts, is too vague to fundamentally diagnose someone such as Ted Bundy. There were clear emotive indicators in place, giving a sense that if a sliding doors scenario had been in place, then things could have had a completely different outcome.

<u>Nature Versus Nurture</u>

<u>Psychopathy or Sociopathic Behaviour?</u>

In Antium, Italy in 12 AD, Gaius was born. Son of the Roman General Germanicus. Gaius was given the name Caligula which translates to "Little Boot". A term borne of affection, given to him by the Roman Soldiers at the front line at Germania in the Roman conquests of the time. Germanicus would bring a young Caligula to the battle front and even went as far as to fashion a military uniform for his young son. The young Caligula witnessed battles and post battle executions while he was at his fathers' side during these wars.

Following the death of his father and a bitter feud between his mother's family with Tiberius (in where Caligula's mother and family were put to death) especially as there were rumours that Tiberius had poisoned Germanicus in a political feud to become Emperor, Caligula, being the sole survivor of his family, was invited to stay at the Island of Capri and was subsequently adopted by the new Emperor Tiberius.

It has been said that Caligula, despite having been spared in the family feud, hated Tiberius. So much so that he had planned to avenge his family's murder and kill Tiberius for himself. Though aware of the dangers that such a folly would place him in, he hid his ambitions well. With both Tiberius and those around him on the Island being completely unaware of Caligula's plans.

While on the island, Caligula was witness to a series of brutality. Tiberius would, for no other reason than his own amusement, throw people that he did not like from the cliffs of the Island. On the island Tiberius had built a vast amount of dungeons, rooms designated for torture, as well as execution areas. All of which Caligula would have been exposed to seeing, as well as the events that unfolded in these places.

Combining Caligula's time that he had spent on the Island of Capri, as well as the brutality of war that he would have been exposed to by his father in Germania, it is very easy to understand just how this type of brutality, as well as just how little the value of human life would have been as a form of learned behaviour. Therefore, it came as quite a surprise when Caligula inherited the position of the Emperor of Rome. Initially, he was deemed to be something of a joyous and generous Emperor. This, however, was not to last.

Following a bout of illness, Caligula seemed to have emerged from his capsule as the magnificent Emperor, as a changed man who was devout on carnage and brutality. Caligula had put to death, any persons who disagreed with his sentiments, even going as far as to instruct the members of his own senate to commit suicide over a period of time. Caligula still seemed the grandiose Emperor to those that were not in direct contact with him. However, all that were in close proximity to him were all subject to his wrath should he have felt the desire to do so. Caligula would use situations in order to manipulate people into getting what he wanted. Should he not get the desired effect, he would simply remind them that he had the power to have them killed. A personality trait that would have been deemed as being an antisocial personality trait, should he have not been in such a high position of power. Further than that, anyone that was deemed to have been conspiring against him, were summarily put to death.

Having control over the life and death of those within his realm was seemingly not enough. There were attempts to conquer and bring brutality to many foreign lands such as Ancient Britain. As well as inviting the leaders of foreign lands to Rome, in where he had these leaders executed. Following these events, there was further evidence of his antisocial tendencies, which by now were mixed in with a form of sexual deviance. In where he would covet the wives of people in high positions, taking them for his own gratification, even going as far as to indulge in sexual relations with his own sister. Again, further evidence that is often accustomed with sexual sadism in Psychopathic or Sociopathic tendencies.

As the Emperor, there was no one that was in a position to either question his decisions, nor his actions. However, in a statement in where he had announced that he had wished to move to Alexandria in Egypt, so that he could be worshipped as a divine entity. The people had had enough. Enough of his reign of brutality, as well as his extreme behaviour towards the senate. He was conspired against and assassinated, much in the same manner that Julius Caesar had been killed, by a series of conspirators stabbing the Emperor. In today's mind, it could be said that the Emperor was put to death for his crimes in a manner which could in itself have been deemed as a private execution. Ironically, having been deemed as an Antisocial Personality type by today's standards, Caligula was put to death on the 24[th of] January 41 AD. The same date in the year in which the infamous Ted Bundy would be put to death almost two thousand years later.

The question that remains unanswered in this scenario, is indeed on of nature versus nurture. Did Caligula inherit his thirst for blood lust and brutality from his general

father, or did he develop this trait as a means
of having been exposed to the front line of
war in Germania and the unspeakable
atrocities that he had witnessed on the
Island of Capri by Tiberius?

Often when a Serial Killer has been
apprehended, the route into discovering
what it was that made the person commit
these crimes, is sourced from their childhood
upbringing. The key factors that become
looked at, would be to understand if there
had been any forms of abuse or neglect,
which may have served as a means as a
catalyst for antisocial behaviour.

It raises the question as to whether or not
the abuse that a Serial Killer had been
subjected to as a child was the ultimate
factor in the victim becoming an abuser
themselves, to then devolving into what we

have come to know as the modern-day Serial Killer. However, should there have been no signs of neglect, it does raise the question that it could be possible that they were just born "bad". The fact that there has been no definitive answer to this question with absolute certainty, leaves the door open that more research and study of Serial Killers is required on the subject.

As per the previous chapter, in the case of Ted Bundy. If you take out of the equation that he was an illegitimate child, having been brought up with the understanding that his mother was actually his sister, there is little to highlight that this was an instrumental factor in his desire to kill. Granted that in that day and age, being an illegitimate child was something that could have been looked at with a degree of scorn. However, for the majority of his formative years, Bundy was unaware of this fact and as such, it would have had little impact on his neurological development.

Other than the fact that he was illegitimate, there was nothing recorded in his youth that would suggest that the lack of nurture from his mother and later, his stepfather, that would lead him on a path to such brutality.

While Ted Bundy is one of the most well-known Serial Killers of the modern age, it would be remiss of the purpose of this book to lay the sole foundation to be based entirely on the psychological mindset of only Ted Bundy. Therefore, comparisons with other Serial Killers will have to be made. The point with using Bundy as a reference in this instance is one of two potential factors. For one, it is not evident that his upbringing played a key role in his ultimate devolution, which would rule out the argument for nurture being the core issue. Yet, studies of his brain following his execution showed no signs of any forms of neurological damage, which would give rise to the theory that the desire to kill did not emanate from any "natural" causes. Giving rise to the theory with regards to Bundy that potentially neither of these factors played a key role with regards to his crimes.

Studies show that up to forty percent of children who have been abused then go on to become violent abusers themselves in later life. In that forty percent of people who have become violent offenders, studies have shown that up to twenty four percent of this category are in fact female perpetrators. Given that the statistics in a global study in 2013, in that it has shown that up to ninety six percent of Serial Killers are male, coupled with the fact that it has shown that up to fifty percent of male Serial Killers had been exposed to either physical or psychological abuse as children. The numbers in support that a lack of nurture being a prevalent factor in propelling a childhood victim into serial murder, are relatively low when compared to the amount of active Serial Killers there are in the world at any given time. Given that the statistics regarding abuse cover all ethnicities and considering that, the vast majority of Serial Killers are in fact, white males between the ages of twenty and thirty-five years old. That percentage of persons from an abusive background devolving into Serial Killers is considerably small in comparison.

So, what is it that has made the high percentage of male children from an abusive background not follow in the same destructive pathway as that of a Serial Killer? Granted that there may been steps taken once abuse in the childhood home had been detected, with a great number of government programs having been put in place to assist the childhood victims of abuse.

It would suggest from these statistics, that the argument for nurture would not be as fundamentally strong for the devolution to serial murder. Naturally, there are exceptions to this theory. In my previous book about Nicolas Claux, the "Vampire of Paris", there was clear indication of emotional neglect during his formative years, which in turn lay down the possibility of a basis for adult Psychosis which devolved into the foundation for his criminal behaviour. Furthermore, if you take the case of Gary Ridgeway, the "Green River Killer", there is evidence to suggest that he suffered emotional abuse and humiliation at the hands of his mother, who would essentially chastise him for being a bed wetter, even up to the age of thirteen. A notion which could have lay the core structure in his anger towards women, who he would ultimately murder over a period of many years.

As stated, this kind of abuse only accounts for a maximum of up to fifty percent of the key indicators in the downward spiral of studied Serial Killers, therefore, the natural inclination would be to suggest that a plausible reason for the devolution to murder would be something that has been damaged in a neurological sense within the individual. There is a possibility of a starvation of oxygen to the brain of a child during birth, or even the possibility of damage to the brain in a childhood accident, which could have hampered the neurological development in the formative years?

In the case of Peter Sutcliffe, also known as the "Yorkshire Ripper". There are no indicators as to any forms of abuse, or in fact, any signs of abnormality from his childhood years. There are no records that I have seen that would suggest that he had suffered any forms of neurological damage in his youth, or even anything to suggest that there were any complications during his birth. So, by all accounts, Sutcliffe's childhood was normal, as well as showing zero key indicators as a youth that he was capable of such deeds.

While continuing with an evaluation of Serial Killers in England. The Infamous Serial Killer known as "Dr Death", Harold Shipman, the Doctor who was rumoured to have been responsible for the deaths of up to one hundred elderly women, in a crime spree which lasted many years in the latter part of the Twentieth Century. Once again, looking at the childhood of Dr Shipman, there was nothing to suggest that his childhood was anything other than normal. In fact, Dr Shipman showed no signs of a destructive nature in his youth, which would have been a key indicator as to his potential future. It was quite the opposite. Dr Shipman had excelled in his time at school, doing well academically and equally so in the sporting field. He was an excellent Rugby player as well as being above average in track and field events. Neurological defects would have perhaps hampered his ability to do so well, not to mention that should there have been any signs of neglect in his formative years, it would have made it quite difficult for Dr Shipman to have become such a success in life at a later time.

It should be noted that in cases of both Dr Shipman and Peter Sutcliffe, that it seems to have been a catalyst stressor which may have started them both on what would turn out to be their separate killing sprees. In the case of Sutcliffe, it could be argued that a degrading and embarrassing sexual encounter with a prostitute in the 1960's, in where he was reportedly conned out of money by the prostitute's pimp, which laid the foundation for his apparent hatred and revenge on prostitution.

With Harold Shipman, he had been very close to his mother. At the age of seventeen Shipman had witnessed the deterioration and death of his mother as a result of lung cancer. During the visits to the Shipman residence by the attending Doctor, the drug Morphine had been administered to his mother as a form of pain relief. The aspect of this that could have been deemed as Shipman's "stressor", would be that witnessing of this drug being administered to his mother, which seemingly became the basis of Shipman's Modus Operandi when it came to the murder of his own victims later in life.

Throughout the history of all Serial Killer cases, it is clearly evident that a series of neglect or abuse, or even both, in some instances, has contributed to some of the serial murder perpetrators devolving to killing at later points in life. Thus, affirming the nurture aspects of a definitive argument in the case of responsibility for eventually committing murder. In the same breath, there is an equal argument that there has been nothing to suggest that the upbringing of a Serial Killer has had any effect on the eventual actions of a killer.

Then of course there is the argument that neither nurture, nor nature has been the fundamental cause for a perpetrator to eventually devolve to the point of taking another person's life. That the sole defining point in where a person has decided to commit murder, especially on a serial basis, has been a key moment in their near adult lives, which has been of enough significance in which their outlook on the world and society has been altered.

It is my conclusion, that neither nurture, nor nature can be taken into account as a definitive cause in these cases. However, in the same breath, it is also vital that they are included at the same time. This statement ultimately seems contradictory; however, it is anything but. My statement is that while it may not be the definitive factor as to why a person may or may not kill, in some cases it could be pivotal, whereas in other cases it may not. It seems as though the profile of every single individual Serial Killer, or even just a person who has committed a solitary murder, should be taken on an individual basis, with all aspects being taken into account. One killer's profile, unless they are a copycat killer, will not be the same as another's.

The concept of nature versus nurture seems to be nothing more than just pieces of a puzzle. It is the individual profile that will determine as to just how big of a puzzle piece those factors are when looking at the picture as a whole.

If the childhood is spent in a manner that would be deemed as out of view for the majority of the family or close circles, such as Caligula while at the frontline of war with his general father or distanced on the Island of Capri with his adoptive peer, Tiberius. Then it is extremely difficult to conclude as to whether nurture or nature was the key factor in his ultimate brutality. Quite possibly, it could ultimately have been both.

<u>Harold Shipman-Tipping the Scales</u>

<u>The Balance between Guilt and Remorse.</u>

Control of an emotion is quite substantial in relation to the ultimate behaviours of a person. Quite often the line becomes blurred in the definition of confusing an emotion and the individual's behaviour. An example of this would be in where a person has spent their afternoon doing some decorating to their home. Only the decorating has not gone as well as they had anticipated. The person feels the constant failings owing to their inadequate DIY skills, finally starting to get the better of them. Only to eventually lose all sense of control and cast out their DIY equipment into the street in what could be described as a fit of rage.

The people who may have encountered this uncouth dumping of the DIY equipment into the street, whether it be their family or friends, state that the unskilled DIY worker has acted out of eventual anger. While the perception of the family member or friend may not be out of context, they are missing one fundamental distinction. They are not acting angrily, but instead are acting out of aggression.

I can imagine that anyone that reading this may question, "What is the difference?" Well in essence, there is quite a big difference. For one, anger is not an action. Anger is an emotion. It is only how well an individual has been able to control this emotion, as how they allow it to affect their actions or behaviours. The behaviour in this instance being aggression.

The same can be said of other emotions, whether it be jealousy, love, sadness, even happiness. All of these emotions have the ability to affect our behaviours, whether it be for a positive or a negative outcome. The key part of what makes these points relevant to someone who is deemed to be a Serial Killer, is that there is evidence that at some stages in their lives, they have not been able to control their emotions, ultimately leading them to crossing the line and committing these horrendous crimes.

The key element in this, however, is the word emotion. If someone who is deemed to have been void of emotion, then how is it possible that they could have reached the stage in where they acted out aggressively, if there was no emotion to lose control of in the first place?

———————————————

For people who have lived in the United Kingdom in the last twenty or so years, there is little chance that they would have looked into the world of Serial Killers or true crime as a genre and not heard of the name Dr Harold Frederick Shipman. Known to his acquaintances as Fred Shipman, but known the to the rest of the world as "Dr Death".

The case relating to Dr Shipman is one that is astounding in terms of the sheer number of victims that this particular Serial Killer has been attributed to. While he was convicted on the 31st of January 2000, for the murders of fifteen elderly patients under his care, it has been estimated by the public that Dr Shipman was responsible for up to one hundred murders, while other sources claim that the number could be as high as two hundred and fifty victims.

As stated in the previous chapter, Dr Shipman had witnessed the family's Doctor administering morphine to his mother, when Shipman was just seventeen years old, for her condition of lung cancer, in which to dull her pain from the symptoms of the cancer. Despite there not being sufficient enough evidence to support the theory that Dr Shipman was inspired by these events, in terms of killing his patients by giving them lethal doses of morphine, it is widely believed that this was the inspiration behind what would later become, his modus operandi.

There does not seem to be an obvious emotional reason for Shipman to have begun his horrendous killings spree, other than greed. For a great deal of his patients, Shipman had forged the last will and testimonies of his victims, so that they would leave sums of money, items of value, and even in some cases, the victim's estate, to Dr Shipman as opposed to the next of kin or family member as was customary. In the beginning, suspicion was not aroused, as it was not uncommon for elderly persons to have left portions of their estate to their local

Doctor, as the family Doctor had quite often treated several generations of a family, often in the family home as opposed to that of a doctor's place of practice. Therefore, as it was common place, especially with patients who did not have many family members left, in which to inherit what remained of a dying person's estate, that sometimes the family Doctor was named as a beneficiary in a person's last will and testimony.

What eventually aroused suspicion was that Shipman had begun to forge the last will and testimonies of persons who still had living family members who would have naturally been the first choice in receiving the inherited estates. Not only were the amounts of the estate that were being left to the Doctor becoming ludicrous in terms of sums of money, but it was becoming more frequent than what would have been deemed as "normal".

Eventually, a family member of a deceased woman, was quite surprised that, upon an elderly family member having passed away, that the entire ownership of the house had been distributed to Dr Shipman in her will, rather than the remaining living relative. This raised alarm within the family and as such, the family requested further inspection of the deceased woman's last will and testimony.

The family had noticed that the last will and testimony had been forged rather crudely in terms of legal documentation. However, initially, the family thought that they were merely arousing nothing more than a case of potential fraud as opposed to a subsequent murder investigation. As with all of Dr Shipman's victims, this woman was elderly and in somewhat of poor health and a frail condition. Therefore, although as sad as the passing away of any person might be, it was not entirely unexpected owing to the age of the persons who were subsequently dying. With this in mind, there was still no reason to suspect that the Doctor was doing anything out the ordinary for his patients.

When the police encountered the potential case of fraud brought to them by the deceased woman's family, the police had no idea as to what they were about to uncover. A closer look at this elderly woman's last will and testimony gave rise to the possibility that this may not be an isolated case of fraud related to Dr Shipman. Further seemingly fraudulent last will and testimonies, inspected by the police, gave cause for concern that they were in fact, dealing with something other than just a few irregularities in terms of legal documentation.

That revelation in terms of what the police discovered about Dr Harold Shipman, turned out to be what could be described by many as the criminal case of a generation. Investigations and further delving into the case histories of some of the patients who had been under his care over the years, concluded that these people had not died of natural causes, with the grounds for more than just suspicion becoming ever more prevalent.

This was not the first time that Dr Harold Shipman had been under the spotlight with the police in the United Kingdom. In 1975, in a town called Todmorden, West Yorkshire, Dr Harold Shipman had been found to have been forging prescriptions of Pethidine (which is a drug in the Demerol family). The prescriptions had been forged so that Shipman was able to obtain the drug for his own use. Instead of being relieved of his medical license, he was fined by the courts for the amount of £600 (Approximately $800) and he went on a drug rehabilitation program in York, North Yorkshire for a short period of time. Following all of this, Dr Shipman then relocated to Hyde, Greater Manchester Area, in which to resume his career as a General Practitioner. It is believed that the majority of Dr Shipman's victims were killed whilst in this role, however, there is reason to believe that he had already begun taking the lives of his patients whilst still in practice in the town of Todmorden. His first victim seemingly having died after being given a fatal dose of morphine by Dr Shipman.

It could have been perceived that Dr Shipman did not forge the last will and testimonies of his initial victims, in that any sums of money that had been left to him as an inheritance by his patients, would have been done so legitimately. Granted that his patients cause of premature death was unscrupulous, however, the fact that he had been named legitimately in his patient's wills', were all standard and above board. It could be argued that a degree of impatience on the part of Dr Shipman, in where he harboured a desire for the day of any potential inheritance to arrive sooner than it would have done under his patients dying of natural causes. It is plausible that a sense of greed was a determining factor in Shipman not only claiming the lives of so many of his patients, but also as to why Dr Shipman then began to forge the last will and testimonies of his patients, so that he would be the primary beneficiary in receiving vast amounts of money and estate.

It is almost beyond comprehension that such an amount of murders was essentially allowed to happen undetected, with Shipman killing at what could be deemed as a merciless rate. Towards the latter part of his career as a Doctor, he had inherited the nickname of "Dr Death" in the community, owing to the fact that so many of his patients were dying in comparison to perhaps other

Doctors in the community. Even with this unwelcomed nickname, there was still little suspicion aroused in terms of actual crime, or in fact, murder. It is fathomable, that should it not have been for his unsatiable greed, even with a reputation for having an extraordinarily high death rate among his patients, that the murderous Doctor may not have been detected for some time.

Therefore, much like Ted Bundy in the sense that he was not apprehended with a direct connection to murder, Bundy having only been apprehended as a result of being pulled over as result of a chance traffic offence while driving erratically at night (On two separate occasions), Dr Shipman's killing spree was only brought to the attention of the relevant authorities as the result of further investigation into claims made against him relating to fraud, an error borne from his ever growing greed for wealth.

In January of 2000, having plead not guilty to fifteen counts of murder, fifteen murders which had been committed between 1995 and 1998. Despite there having been a suspicion that Shipman had killed many more victims dating back to as far as 1975, there was only sufficient evidence to convict Dr Shipman on these fifteen particular cases. Shipman was sentenced to fifteen life sentences in prison, without him ever having the possibility of being released.

The life sentences, would ultimately turn out to have been futile in nature, owing to the fact that Dr Shipman would only ever serve approximately four years in prison in total. The reason for this being that, on the 13th of February 2004, Dr Harold Ship took his own life in his prison cell by ripping up his bed sheets so that he was able to hang himself to death. Following a post mortem examination and short inquest into Dr Shipman's death, no conclusion as to why the Doctor may have decided to end his own life in the manner in which he had.

The absence of a suicide note led to wide speculation as to the motives for the Doctor's decision to end his own life. It had been rumoured that Dr Shipman had informed his probation officer of his intentions to commit suicide so that the £100,000 (approximately $136,000) life insurance policy that he had in place would be able to be paid to his wife of thirty-eight years.

Following Shipman's suicide, it has been reported that whilst in prison, the convicted Doctor had refused to take part in courses which would have seen him acknowledge his crimes to the authorities. For me, this raises more questions than it answers. While a series of Serial Killers, even after having been convicted, refuse to acknowledge their crimes out of a sense of wishing to have their guilt overturned by the court of appeals (Ted Bundy did this as well), it is worth noting that I have not been able to locate any evidence that appeals of this nature had been lodged by the imprisoned Dr Shipman. In fact, there is only the rumour that Shipman had made any statement with regards to making an appeal on his sentences, just days before his decision to have taken his own life.

This opens up the possibility for a great deal more questioning in terms of the mindset of Dr Harold Shipman. As stated previously, there was nothing in Dr Shipman's history regarding his earlier life that would have given indication as to any forms of Antisocial Personality Disorders. Yet any person that has been able to commit such a vast number of murders must surely be void of any human emotions? This is where the potential theory that these emotions do exist within the mindset of certain Serial Killers.

Shipman has been noted to have been very close to his mother in his formative years. There are no indicators to show that he was anything other than a loving son, who could have been deemed as a model child and even adolescent. Therefore, if Shipman was cable of love towards his mother, then surely, he was capable of other emotions as well? It is fair to state that Dr Shipman was in fact fuelled by greed. Greed essentially being one of the Christian fundamental "seven deadly cardinal sins". In where greed details the covetousness of another's attributes or possessions. Greed can be deemed as a powerful, if not negatively orientated emotion, however, it is a human emotion, nonetheless.

Dr Shipman's suicide could also, upon delving into further possibilities, be linked to the recognition of a person who is not void of human emotion. In one way of looking at his decision to take his own life, in where he already knew that subjects of a financial nature were not going to be one of his ultimate concerns, given that he was going to spend the remainder of his natural life inside of a prison cell. Therefore, in a sense, his financial issues were no longer an issue for Shipman. If what was said to his probation officer has any truth to it, then he was thinking about the financial situation that his wife, Primrose Shipman, was going to be left in. Therefore, in a fashion, the taking of his own life would be the final selfless action that he could have done, ensuring that his wife of thirty-eight years, was not going to have to endure the stress of financial hardship going forward. The love and thoughts in relation to his wife is something that superseded the importance of even his own life at this point in time. A potential gesture which could not have been carried out, should there be an absence of human emotion.

The alternative theory when considering the suicide of Dr Shipman, is that, especially when it is taken into consideration that the Doctor had refused to participate in groups which would have seen him taken the moral responsibility for his murders, that he was not open to receiving any forms of therapy, which could have led to the moral absolution within himself for what he had done to his patients. It is common knowledge that bottling up the guilt or emotions relating to problems in life, has the possibility of leaving a person unable to deal with their own guilt and other emotions. With the ability to extend his criminal activity for the purposes of acquiring wealth in relation to his unsatiable greed, there was no longer any reason for the convicted Doctor to have greed in the forefront of his mindset.

In his four years of sitting in his prison cell, with nothing to occupy his mind other than the memories of the potentially hundreds of victims that he had claimed the lives of, it is quite plausible that after a period of time, that the guilt for his actions had become too much for his mind to be able to deal with any longer. Especially when considering that he had not allowed himself the outlet of releasing his guilt in any forms of possible therapy. It is not beyond the realms of reasonable thought that, the guilt of his actions just became too much for the imprisoned Doctor, so much so that he felt that the only way to escape his guilt, was to end his own life.

While many people viewed the Doctor as nothing more than a callous monster, this lays the foundation that despite never wanting to admit publicly to his crimes, the guilt and remorse for his actions was not something that he was able to overcome. The faces of his victims, potentially haunting his thoughts and dreams, to the point in where the only way to escape it, was to end his own life. This does not mean that Dr Shipman was not the monster that people in the public, or even the families of his victims had perceived him to be, however, it lays the plausibility that despite being what could be deemed as a psychotic killer, the potential for remorse in the convicted Doctor was present. Meaning that he was not void of human emotion.

This is of course, merely speculative, as the only way that we would ever have known the workings of the inner mind of Dr Harold Shipman, would have been to have heard the words directly from his own mouth. Owing to the fact that he has now passed away, the final statement that was made, was in a sense, by the taking of his own life, a statement made without ushering a single spoken word. A statement which allows us to claim our own understanding, albeit all by our own individual means of speculation.

We will never know just what emotions Dr Shipman felt, although in my mind, a remorseless and guilt free person, who cares of nothing other than his own gratification, in my opinion, would but for the reasons of natural causes, still be in prison today.

John Wayne Gacy

A clown emerges from the cinders.

It is not a common occurrence in that I am able to make an analogy out of something as innocent as a children's fairy-tale, however, for the purposes of what shall become clarified later in the chapter, I ask that you indulge me for the moment.

We look into the story of Cinderella, a young girl born into what is, the potential for a happy life, yet owing to the nature of her family, finds herself having a lifestyle of hardship and seeming disappointment in terms of gaining recognition and approval. A life that in the end, takes a turn for the positive, finding a means to put an end to their miserable existence, by leading what seems to be a double life from her family and home life. In Cinderella's eyes, the alternate life is indulgent and considerably more grandiose. After a period of time, the life that was hidden becomes the life that she becomes known for, with the lasting memory of her secondary life becoming what she is ultimately remembered for.

It all sounds incredibly positive in nature, however, if you were to reverse the positive aspects of this story, it would not have been seen as a fairy-tale, but instead, as a story built on the realms of tragedy.

The use of the story of Cinderella does not, however, end there. There is one more factor which could have been seen as being increasingly significant. That being the factor of the glass slipper. The glass slipper was tried on by many a young girl, however, it was only possible for it to ever fit one person's foot, that being Cinderella herself. The glass slipper may have had many fitting similarities to the features of other young girls' feet; however, it was only ever going to fit Cinderella in perfect unison.

In the same manner, a psychological diagnosis made in terms of people who commit serial murders, it is not always going to fit every person who is suspected of these types of killings. There may be similarities and common traits in where we are led to believe that a diagnosis might fit, yet there can be things missing which lead us to believe that it is not perfect.

Sometimes, the diagnosis can be an absolute perfect fit, much in the same fashion as the glass slipper was the perfect fit for Cinderella. The diagnosis of the Antisocial Personality Disorder is seemingly the perfect fit for one John Wayne Gacy.

John Wayne Gacy was born in Chicago, Illinois, in March of 1942. He was brought up by his parents, his mother being a loving and nurturing home maker, while his father was a strict, masculine orientated World War One veteran, who went on to become an Auto Machine machinist. Gacy had two sisters.

While Gacy was close to his mother and his two sisters, his father was an alcoholic who seemingly was abusive to the young John Wayne Gacy, with quite a degree of frequency. The fact that Gacy was overtly close to his mother, gave him the reputation that he was a "momma's boy" and the rumours around the local town that there was a high degree of probability that Gacy would grow up to be a homosexual. His father, being regarded as something of a "man's man", took displeasure in seeing the seeming lack of masculinity in his son and therefore, used this displeasure, coupled by alcohol intoxication, to beat his son, almost as though it was done in a manner in which to attempt to toughen him up a bit.

Gacy was unable to excel in any forms of sport, due to a medical condition of suffering seizures, another thing that his father was not shy in displaying his displeasure for. There was always a fear of "not being good enough" by a young Gacy, in his father's eyes, therefore, in his youth, out of fear of not wishing to disappoint his father, he felt as though he could not confide in his father when he had been sexually molested by a local contractor and family friend.

Despite having to live with the torment of having been sexually molested as a child, as well as the constant views of disapproval in the eyes of his father. Gacy went on to become involved in politics with a local political party. This once again was met with disapproval from his father. It has been said that John Wayne Gacy, despite having received very little in terms of approval from his father, still loved him dearly, however, as the young man was not gaining any forms of approval from his own father, he opted for seeking the recognition he desired from others instead.

Shortly into his young adult life, John Wayne Gacy left Chicago and made his was to Las Vegas, Nevada, in search of starting a new life for himself, away from the disapproving eyes of his father. In Las Vegas, Gacy was able to obtain a job working as an ambulance driver, before then leaving the ambulances to go and work in a local mortuary, working as a cleaner in the building. Gacy worked for three months in the mortuary, having observed the morticians working with the deceased bodies while carrying out his cleaning duties.

There were times in where Gacy would have been left alone within the mortuary. As such, Gacy has admitted that during one of these times of solitude, he decided to climb inside of the coffin of a deceased teenage boy. Gacy has admitted to having caressed the corpse of the young man, before awaking from what he was doing in what he describes as a sense of shock. This sense of shock ultimately led to the understanding that it was time for him to return to his home in Chicago.

Upon his return to Chicago, it can be said that Gacy's life had taken a turn for the positive. He had enrolled in college, trying to develop his, until then, unsuccessful schooling career. Gacy started to do well in this respect, not only that, but having made progression in his academic life, these progressions managed to manifest themselves in other aspects of his life. Gacy had begun life in the working world, he worked at a shoe company, in where he eventually rose to become a manager. These working successes had a knock-on effect in his personal life, as while working in the shoe company, he met, and soon married, co-worker Marlynn Myers. A woman whom he would go on to have two children with. In addition to his social and work-related successes, Gacy had taken on a role at a local development program, a civic organisation which was set up with the ideals of offering training programmes for people in the community between the ages of eighteen and forty.

The success that Gacy had in life in terms of both work and establishing a family life, ultimately brought with it, the one thing that John Wayne Gacy had longed for, for the entirety of his life, that being the approval from his domineering father. His father had finally said to the successful Gacy, the words that he had longed to hear, that he had in fact been wrong about his son.

This new found success for Gacy was not without its own forms of secrecy and times of confusion. Not only had he kept his experience to himself regarding his interactions with the corpse of the deceased teenage boy whilst working in Las Vegas, but further to this, there had been further homosexual experiences which Gacy had kept away from the seeing eyes of his personal life. During a drinking session with members of the Civic training organisation, one of the male members of the organisation had gotten Gacy intoxicated, to which he convinced Gacy to allow him to have oral sex performed on him. This would certainly have created a degree of confusion within the ever-developing mind of John Wayne Gacy.

The Gacy family then moved to Waterloo, Illinois, in where Gacy continued his aspiring career by taking on the position of manager for three KFC stores which were owned by his spouse's family. Gacy did well in this role, becoming key in developing each of the stores. Gacy employed both men and women in each of the three KFC stores, however, it has been said that Gacy would interact with mainly the males under his employ, to be more specific, it was the younger males that Gacy was noticed to have paid the most attention to.

In 1967, things would take a turn for the worse in terms of the ever-growing world that John Wayne Gacy had built up for himself. An incident occurred in which would lead to the destruction of not only his career, but also his marriage, with Gacy ultimately being sent to prison. Gacy had brought a fifteen-year-old boy named Donald Voorhees, back to his home under the pretence that he was willing to show the fifteen-year-old boy, pornographic videos. Whilst at the house, Gacy managed to ply the fifteen-year-old boy with enough alcohol to have lowered his inhibitions enough in where he agreed to perform oral sex on Gacy. Following this ill-fated night, Gacy was rumoured to have enacted this same repetiteur on other unsuspecting young males, however, it was the case pertaining to Voorhees that was brought to the authorities, which subsequently led to the arrest and imprisonment of John Wayne Gacy.

Before trial, Gacy was ordered to undergo Psychiatric evaluation, in where he was diagnosed as having an Antisocial Personality Disorder, with Psychopathic or Sociopathic tendencies. Following this, Gacy was determined to competent to stand trial, in which he was found guilty and sentenced to ten years imprisonment, however, he would ultimately only serve eighteen months of this sentence due to his valued work in the prison kitchens, as well as his ability to influence other prison inmates to cooperate in the ongoing prison training programmes.

Gacy was released from prison, all the while maintaining his innocence for the crime in which he had been convicted of. However, there was no end in sight for Gacy's troubles, or indeed his criminal implications. Gacy had not been out of prison long when he was to be once again forced to appear in court, having been charged with sexual assault on yet another young boy. The charges only being eventually dropped owing to the fact that the young man who had accused him of the sexual assault not actually appearing to the courtroom in order to testify against him.

This was not an isolated incident, as the following year, similar charges were filed against Gacy for sexual misconduct against another young boy, only for the charges to eventually be dropped as a result of the court's discovery that the accuser had used the impending court charges as a means to try and attempt to blackmail the defending Gacy. Despite the charges being dropped on both occasions, there was a sinister trend beginning to formulate. The fact that his parole board did not hear of these charges against him until the end of his parole period, was paramount in ensuring that Gacy was not mandated to have his parole revoked. Following the end of his probation period, his initial records pertaining to his first conviction, were sealed by the courts.

Gacy then moved to his infamous address at West Summerdale Avenue, a house that he was able to purchase with the financial assistance of his mother. Gacy's life once again began to show positive signs of promise. He was active in the local community, with the vast majority of the community completely unaware of his deviant history and subsequent criminal conviction. He had gotten married once again and moved his new wife and stepchildren into his newly acquired property. All the while, however, there was a sinister undercurrent which was continuing to flow beneath the seemingly happy Gacy household. After some time, Gacy had admitted to his new wife that he was in fact bisexual, to which the pair had agreed to petition for divorce, despite continuing to live under the same roof at West Summerdale Avenue.

During this time, Gacy started to bring teenage boys to the basement in his house, in which to engage in homosexual activity. While it is not suspected that any murders had been committed during this period of time, the bringing back of numbers of young boys were solely for the purposes of sex. After a short while, his estranged wife and Gacy finalised their divorce and she and her daughters, moved out of the house in West Summerdale Avenue.

Outside of his home life, Gacy was seen to have been thriving in the community. He had started a construction business which seemed to prosper. In addition to this, Gacy was doing volunteer work in where he would visit fundraising events set up with the aim of raising money for hospitalised children, in where he had dressed up for the occasion, by creating the character of "Pogo the Clown". Gacy often stated that although he had been dressing up as the clown in order to assist with the welfare of hospitalised children, it further allowed him to regress back to his childhood, which according to Gacy's history, may not have been deemed as a positive aspect should the people that he was making the statement to have been aware of his troubled past.

The "Pogo the Clown" moniker was not, however, restricted to only fundraising and welfare events, as it became evident that Gacy was starting to incorporate this character into his home life. It is understood that Gacy would bring young boys back to his home, ply them with alcohol, to which he would then offer to show them a "magic trick". This magic trick comprised of Gacy convincing his alcohol fuelled companion to agree to be placed in handcuffs. To which Gacy would then depart the room with his companion bound in handcuffs, while he transformed himself into the "Pogo the Clown" character. The difference in this particular transformation into his clown costume was that there was nothing to suggest that the clown that reappeared was anything at all like the playful and friendly clown that would appear at children's events.

It has been stated that Gacy would, while in his clown character, attempt to chase his handcuffed victim around the room, making exclamations in a high-pitched tone, that his intention was that he was going to rape them. At least this is the testimony that was given by a victim who had managed to survive his antics.

Gacy would lure young boys back to his home and it was here that Gacy killed his vast amount of victims. He would murder them in his home and then dispose of their bodies in the crawl space underneath his own house. It has been reported that a number of Gacy's victims had in fact been employees of his construction firm.

Gacy is considered to have committed his killing spree from 1972 until 1978. A six-year killing spree which is believed to have claimed the lives of thirty-three victims. There was suspicion surrounding his crimes before he had actually been apprehended, however, Gacy was able to evade arrest for a considerable period of time, before he was finally arrested and convicted on the 22nd of March 1980. The jury had only required two hours in which to deliberate in finding Gacy guilty of all of the counts in which he had been charged. Given that the death penalty had been reintroduced in Illinois in 1977, Gacy was sentenced to death for his crimes.

While it is true that the details of events which unfolded between the time that Gacy had moved into West Summerdale Avenue and the time of subsequent conviction for the spate of murder that he had committed, are horrific. However, it is relevant as to just how his behaviour during these events fitted in within the parameters of his diagnosis of an Antisocial Personality Disorder, which was given to him at the time he was first convicted of sexual assault in 1967.

This particular diagnosis seemed to be a perfect fit in terms of Gacy's character. Especially when Gacy's childhood is taken into consideration. The fact that he had suffered physical and mental abuse at the hands of his father at a young age, was paramount to his development during his formative years. Progressing into adolescence, it is clear that Gacy had been struggling with his own sexuality, yet given the masculine doctrines that had been set forth by his domineering father, coupled with the physical abuse that Gacy had suffered at his hand, there was not a comfortable or healthy environment in where Gacy would have been free to discover his sexual orientation in a healthy and less destructive manner.

This clearly had an impact on how his mind functioned as he became a young adult, being an example of Gacy understanding his sexuality to be something of a form of taboo. Therefore, dipping his toes in the water of something deemed to be "unthinkable", meant that there was going to be little distinction from one taboo to another.

Something that has been displayed in the actions of Gacy having caressed the corpse of a teenage boy whilst working at the mortuary in his younger life.

It seems as though the foundation for his ultimate diagnosis had been set in what would have been these formative years, with there being little prospects for a positive recovery. If the words of Gacy are to be believed, he has confessed to having committed his first murder at the age of fifteen. At this stage in his life, Gacy would not have been even remotely developed in terms of neurological progression, therefore, if an act of murder at such a young age is true, then the concept of killing would have been something as normal to Gacy as something that a person without this diagnosis would deem to be, such as, going on holiday for example. Thus, making the concept of killing to Gacy, not something that would trigger an adverse emotional response within him, as murder was part of his neurological consistencies.

When Gacy had left the family home and moved to Las Vegas, he had managed to get a job entirely by his own merit, which would have given Gacy not only the means in which he knew that he could support himself, but also the mindset that when he fends for himself in the outside world, he had the ability to be successful in doing so. This ability not only served him well when he initially went to prison for sexual assault, but also when he was subsequently released and began his series of jobs and careers, especially in Chicago.

Gacy had managed to conceal his sexually deviant tendencies from the other inmates whilst he was in prison, as well as managing to conceal them from the people that he was employed by upon his release. To the

majority of the outside world, Gacy was just
a normal, likeable person, who fitted into
public view almost seamlessly, however, all
the while his deviant undercurrent
continued to flow beneath the surface. Gacy
had the ability to be coercive, manipulative,
and even deceitful in order to obtain what he
wanted in not only his professional life, but
also in terms of his deviant alternate
personal life. It was as though he was living
in parallel worlds, excelling in his career(s)
and excelling in coercing young boys to
come back to his house to engage in his
sexual desires.

Gacy had an adaptive personality, after
having been convicted in the past for sexual
misconduct, to then having been brought
under the spotlight for similar actions on
other young men and boys, it could be said
that the devolution to the murdering of his
victims was so that there would be no form
of witness in which to potentially

incriminate him for his sexual misconduct. Not only has there never been any signs of remorse from Gacy in terms of showing emotion towards his victims, but when he ultimately gave his confession to the police regarding the murdered victims, Gacy dismissed his victims as being nothing more than male prostitutes, hustlers, and liars. Giving clear indication that Gacy thought of his victims as nothing more than a sub-species, which were not deserving of any forms of sympathy or remorse.

In addition, Gacy can be viewed as being of a narcissistic personality. All that he had done had been for his own gratification, with little thought towards those around him. His marriages', especially his second marriage left his wife and her two children searching for a new home, owing to the fact that Gacy was more concerned with indulging his own sexual deviance rather than being committed to his family development. While his dressing up as "Pogo the clown" could have been deemed as positive in terms of the fundraising that he had done for children, he himself had admitted that he had done the transformation into the clown as it allowed him to regress back to his childhood. Considering that Gacy utilised the same character of "Pogo" in both of his charity work, as well as his killing activities, it is an indication that the "Pogo the clown" character, was not for the benefit of others, but done so, more in the mindset of gratifying his own needs and desires more than anything else.

Narcissism can quickly evolve into that of arrogance if it is not managed in the correct manner. This can be clearly seen with the case of Gacy. The fact that he continued to indulge himself in his sexual deviance, despite having two separate sets of charges brought against him following his initial release from prison, did nothing to quell the narcissism within. It could be argued that Gacy had begun to believe that he was beyond reprisals from the authorities, as a search warrant for his property brought insufficient evidence in which he could be charged for. The police continued to place surveillance on Gacy, yet rather than heed the warning, Gacy instead brought a civil action against the police, to not only attempt to put a stop to the surveillance, but also to attempt to gain compensation of $750,000 for his troubles. Naturally, there were still suspicions regarding Gacy's guilt in relation to the local missing boys and as such, the surveillance on him was to not cease. However, on one fateful night, Gacy's arrogance led him to approaching the surveying police officers and inviting them into his home for dinner.

This proved to be a fatal mistake. Gacy had been burying the bodies of his victims in the crawl space of his house, using lime as a means in which to speed up the decomposition process. Gacy's arrogance in terms of inviting in the police officers is a clear sign of his heightened narcissism. The police officers could not help but notice the foul smell which was emanating from the crawl space of the house, a factor which was key in terms of obtaining a second search warrant for the property. A fate which ultimately led to the discovery of the bodies and Gacy's subsequent arrest and conviction.

Even as John Wayne Gacy sat on death row, he maintained that he was not entirely homosexual, a key window into the mindset that he had still not recovered from the oppressive views of his father that had come to be instilled within Gacy from a young age. Further to this, another key factor that there has been no neurological development in terms of remorse or emotional connection, was rather than to be ashamed of his antics, he almost seemed to revel in them, by the observation of the topic of the paintings that Gacy had done while on death row. That being, his paintings of himself as the character of "Pogo the clown". Clearly, there was a sense of reminiscence in Gacy's paintings, creating the understanding that Gacy, even at the latter stages of his life, seen nothing negative in what he had done.

John Wayne Gacy left this world in rebellious fashion. Despite being given the opportunity in his last words to atone for his crimes, instead he chose the timely words of "Kiss my Ass!" Another sign showing that Gacy clearly showed no remorse.

The exercise in telling the tale of John Wayne Gacy, is not one to prove that Serial Killers have no ability in which to show remorse or emotion. Rather it is to cover the aspects of the Antisocial Personality Disorder, or even in fact, any Psychiatric diagnosis. There are far too many indicators that a blanket diagnosis is not going to be a complete fit for all serial murderers, therefore, it is important that a diagnosis of such broad possibility is taken on individual merit. However, as with the case of Cinderella and the glass slipper, sometimes it will be the perfect fit, such as the case with John Wayne Gacy. In this instance, there was nothing to indicate that he was able to feel or show remorse, therefore there was no real potential for rehabilitation.

It seems in this instance, that the diagnosis of an Antisocial Personality Disorder was in fact, John Wayne Gacy's very own glass slipper.

The Death Penalty

Eyes wide shut or unable to see?

The ability to educate oneself is a precious commodity to have in not only modern times, but also when taking a look at the behaviours of people in a retrospective fashion.

The saying that history repeats itself is a phrase which is commonly used, and it is quite often historical behaviours which are used by analysts when predicting the potential outcomes of things such as financial markets. Even companies such as supermarkets and wholesalers use historical trends to determine how much stock that they need to order, so that there are no shortages at particular times of the year, when looking back at shopping trends over previous years.

So why is it when we have professionals hired by marketing companies in order to predict the behaviour of people in terms of public spending, often with a wide degree of success, can we not apply this same strategy of studying human behaviour, to the types of people who eventually devolve into becoming Serial Killers.

I fully appreciate that psychologists and psychiatrists have spent many a year studying the patterns in the human mind, in terms of psychopathy and sociopathy, to which their findings have been filtered down to professionals such as criminal profilers and local police stations, as well as to even a more grass roots level, such as child counsellors and even to a degree, school teachers, so that they can identify problematic issues and be able to do something about these issues before they are able to devolve into more serious and substantial problems that develop in later adult life.

Yet, despite these finding being filtered down, we are still finding that the issue of serial murder is not yet something that has been confined to history. It is reported that in the United States alone, there are reports that up to at least two hundred Serial Killers are still active in today's society. Does that mean that the current system of identifying these potential traits have failed? Or it is merely a subject that we have not fully mastered as of yet?

The subject of the Death Penalty is, and has always been, one that stirs up a great deal of divisive opinion and controversy. Not only in places such as the United States, but in all free-thinking countries that still have the Death Penalty as a form of Capital Punishment. While anti-death penalty groups campaign year after year to countries such as China, Belarus, The United States and Saudi Arabia, internationally condemning this form of Capital Punishment. However, there are still people and authorities who stand by this form of punishment for offenders who are deemed to be beyond rehabilitation.

Therefore, the possibility of the debate being brought to any forms of conclusion, one way or the other, is unlikely to being closer to resolution in the near future. Whilst China have refused to provide the figures for the number of state executions to organisations such as Amnesty International, it is believed that China has been responsible for the highest number of executions in recent years, followed by Iran, Saudi Arabia, Iraq, and Egypt. The offences for which the punishment of execution from countries such as these, remain varied and to a degree, vague when compared to places such as the United States.

In the United Kingdom, Capital Punishment has been all but eradicated. Since 1965, the Murder (Abolition of Death Penalty) Act was brought in to replace the Homicide Act of 1957, in where the Death Penalty could only be utilised for the crimes of Treason, Piracy with Violence, Espionage, and Arson within Royal Dockyards. In fact, the sentence for these crimes being that execution was mandatory unless the sentence had been commuted by the Monarch. However, in 1998, the United Kingdom changed the laws regarding these crimes to implement the sentence of Life Imprisonment, making the U.K a fully abolished country in terms of Capital Punishment. Such a change was then encouraged for other countries to follow suit, such as the United States.

In the United States, the amount of people who have been executed by either the Federal Government, or by the individual state, has decreased significantly in recent years, with some states within the country, even going as far as to abolish the death penalty in its entirety. However, there are still states such as Florida, California, Arizona, and Texas who still carry out Capital Punishment. The amount of executions which are undertaken each year, varies vastly depending on who in fact the Governor of each state is at the time of signing the resulting death warrants. It has been argued that the United States, being an ex-colonial state of the United Kingdom, had followed suit in inheriting the, what was current implementation of punishment from the very country they fought to be liberated from. However, the United States are now being encouraged to follow in suit in the example of abolishment of this punishment, from what is considered to be their "mother land".

The debate regarding the death penalty is not one that is going to be resolved overnight, especially when taken into account the considerable amount of time that inmates on the United States Death Row, spend as an average fourteen and a half years awaiting their execution. The reason for this being that the prisoner who has been condemned to death has to go through the series of the appeals processes and only once these sets of appeals have been exhausted, can the final death warrant be signed, and an execution date be determined. This process brings with it a varied set of complications. Quite often, when the date of execution finally arrives, the families of the victims, even though some of which are generally happy that the perpetrator is having justice delivered, all have to, in a sense re-live the circumstances which brought about the need to a trial by court in the first place.

For some, it is a case of being allowed the closure in which to heal, however, for others, it is an awakening of grief and a sense of their emotional wounds being opened up once again. A notion which some families find all too painful to go through again.

Without sounding ambiguous, as I live in a country (U.K) which does not have the Death Penalty for capital crimes, nor have I been faced with the horrendous situation of having a family member having fallen victim to a crime which would see the death penalty being deemed worthy of such a form of punishment. Therefore, if you take the emotional aspect of the Death Penalty away, then I must admit that I do not have a foundation, nor a solid opinion as to whether capital punishment is the correct basis for social nirvana. Therefore, for the purposes of the reasons which I aim to discuss going forward, I am going to do so without bringing personal emotion to the discussion.

If you take the moral dilemma in which the implementation of the Death Penalty brings, out of the equation, then there are other factors which seem to raise concerns. As I understand it, the fundamental reasoning behind not only Capital Punishment, but indeed any forms of incarceration, are not being done by the courts as a form of punishment. From what I have read on various government websites, the implementation of a prison sentence should only be utilised when there are no other forms of rehabilitation that are viable in its place. Therefore, creating the alternative that in the cases of diminished mental capacity for example, a prison sentence would not be seen as suitable form of rehabilitation, as such, a period of time in a facility such as hospital designated for the criminally insane, is better suited to adhere to the needs of the individual in terms of the correct rehabilitation.

As it stands, especially in places such as the United States, the implementation of the Death Penalty for crimes such as murder, or even sexually assault based murder, is given to the individual perpetrator when it has been deemed by the judge (on the recommendation of the jury in a lot of cases) that the perpetrator has been deemed to fall beyond the parameters of being able to be rehabilitated. As opposed to, but quite often is viewed as, being a punishment for the crime that they have been convicted of.

For me, this raises more questions than it tends to answer. The first being that, I would hope, that the presiding judge, takes an educated and informed opinion from that of a team of psychological and neurological professionals, as to whether the person being sentenced to death, is capable of change. Granted that does not mean that, given their crimes, they would ever be in a position in which they could be trusted enough in which to re-enter the free world again. However, even if there is no grounds or basis of ever being released, it does not necessarily mean that they could not perform some form of useful function whilst still being held in incarceration. In recent history, there has always been the thought process that a person who was spending years behind bars, was subjected to the chores of having to crunch out motor vehicle license plate numbers. Granted that this could be seen to some as a mundane task, however, in a fashion, the prisoner in question was still able to provide some sort of a service to the outside public. I am sure that with enough research, there would be no shortages of ways a prisoner who was spared the penalty of death, whilst not maintaining any real possibility of future release, could not have a way discovered for them, in which they would be able to find some forms of public service, even if it meant it was done without having contact with said public.

The two examples which have been used in this book thus far would be two perfect examples of polar opposites in terms of this argument being put forward in this scenario. Firstly, if we take the case of John Wayne Gacy, whom the story of in the previous chapter was based upon. If there is a widespread agreement as to the nature of Gacy's crimes having been committed without any forms of remorse and that, Gacy fits in with almost absolute certainty that he is the stereotypical example of a person diagnosed with an Antisocial Personality Disorder, then there can be little argument as to the sentence of Death as a form of Capital Punishment being handed down. (Provided a consensus of being pro Capital Punishment is agreed upon for this argument).

With Gacy, despite having spent many years on Death Row (approximately fourteen years in total). Even as he took his final steps towards his execution, never showed even the slightest morsel of remorse towards his victims. Especially when Gacy's final words of "Kiss my Ass", were his last stand in defiance of him thinking that he had done nothing wrong. Therefore, it can be deduced that the penalty of death for his crimes could have been seen as appropriate, given that there would have been very little that could have been done in which to rehabilitate John Wayne Gacy with any forms of hope or success. Making the argument for sparing Gacy's life null and void in this scenario.

On the opposite side of the equation, when we look at the life and crimes of Ted Bundy, we have crimes that, just like Gacy, were horrific in nature and stirred up a sense of disbelief in the public in the United States at their respective given times. The similarities do not end with the fact that they both committed heinous crimes, but in fact, both of these Serial Killers met their demise at the hands of state recruited executioners. So where are the fundamental differences between these two separate Serial Killers?

For the vast majority of his time that he had spent on Florida's death row, Ted Bundy had maintained his innocence. Even going as far as to refuse to speak in the first person when interviewed by Aynesworth and Michaud in their book ***Ted Bundy: Conversation with a killer***. It was only in the final days of his life in where Bundy eventually admitted to the authorities that he was in fact responsible for the crimes that he had been convicted of. Even placing his hopes of a last-minute reprieve on the possibility that his executioners would give him a stay of execution in exchange for information relating to the whereabouts of the undiscovered victims of his crimes.

This was an offer in which the authorities had declined to accept and as a result, Bundy was set to be taken to the execution chamber as scheduled. Following the knowledge that Bundy's stay of execution had failed, Bundy then proceeded to engage in what would be his final interview with the Rev Dr James Dobson, as covered in a previous chapter.

As stated previously, it can be seen in this interview with Rev Dr Dobson, that Ted Bundy was seen to have displayed remorse for his crimes, as well as admitting that he was in fact guilty. I fully appreciate that his signs of remorse and admission of guilt only came to be in the final stages of his incarceration, however, as the saying goes "better late than never".

It is unclear as whether or not Ted Bundy had developed a sense of remorse over a period of time, or if his remorse had been within him throughout the times of his murderous exploits. Taking reference once again from Aynesworth and Michaud's book in relation to his "third party recollections", Bundy has been quoted as saying that, once a sexual assault had taken place and the subsequent silencing of the victim, by way of murder, there would have been an adjustment period following the murder, in which the "third party" would have needed to process what had happened, to deal with the emotions that the murder had manifested. As to suggest that before any sexually motivated desires became the forefront of the perpetrators train of thought once more, it was a case of having to come to terms with, and "deal with" the emotions from the previous attack. It is these words which lead me to believe that an emotional reaction, possibly even remorse, could have been present at the times of the murders and not just in Bundy's final interview with Rev Dr Dobson.

If there was in fact evidence of remorse from Bundy, then it leans towards the suggestion that Ted Bundy may in fact have had the ability in which to rehabilitate to a degree. It has been shown that Bundy relished in his unorthodox "family life" with Carole Anne Boone, the woman whom he had married while facing a separate murder trial in Orlando, Florida, for the murder of Kimberly Leach.

There is no suggestion in any of this that Ted Bundy would ever have been deemed as suitable for release from prison, however, there is enough evidence of remorse in both Ted Bundy's words and actions, that a potential for rehabilitation was possible. Thus, by the definition of sentencing of Capital Crimes, there was sufficient enough evidence that his being sentenced to death could have been overturned. To be replaced by a potential sentence of life imprisonment, without the possibility of parole.

Looking at the Bundy case as a form of research into the psychological mindset of a killer. It could be argued that the blanket diagnosis of being an Antisocial Personality Disorder, would therefore not fit the mental state of Bundy in its entirety. Therefore, it could be suggested that the full extent of understanding the mind of a convicted killer such as Ted Bundy, was not done to its full potential. For as many answers that the Bundy case raises, there are still so many questions that remain unanswered.

Therefore, it is entirely plausible that until the full extent of Ted Bundy's mindset had been fully evaluated, then it would have been negligent to close the case by giving him a blanket diagnosis when there was still so much that could have been learned. Conducting these studies would have not brought any of his victims back from the dead, however, it could have provided more insight into a character such as Bundy, with the information that was gathered being collated, studied, and used to proper purpose so that lives of future victims of a Serial Killer of a similar nature could have been prevented at an earlier stage.

The potential decision to take Ted Bundy off of Death Row and replace his sentence to that of life imprisonment, would not have been a popular one in many people's eyes, especially when you take into account the seemingly carnival atmosphere that was evident outside of the Florida prison in the days surrounding his execution. However, keeping Ted Bundy alive so that he could be analysed and studied, even if it were only after he had made his notorious confessions to Rev Dr Dobson, would still have provided a significantly more amount of time in where answers could have been gained and utilised as a means to assist preventing future crimes as a whole.

It seems as though the sparing of one life, from the punishment of execution, is outweighed by the potential to save many more in terms of potential victims in the future. In the study of Ted Bundy, this was not going to be the case. The argument still exists as to the usefulness of the death penalty, however, with Ted Bundy having been put to death, despite the horrific nature of his crimes, there are no questions from his case that will be able to provide possible answers.

Historical research in terms of speculation comes when studies are conducted and information is gathered, much in the same fashion as marketing companies gather information. Without the extended information, there is little chance to study the trends, or even indeed base a fundamental speculation as to what people will do next. With regards to this subject, it does add fuel to the fire in terms of whether or not the death penalty really works or is it just a case of closing our eyes so that certain evils are not only out of sight, but out of mind as well.

<u>Kings to Street Sweepers.</u>

<u>Who's considered to be the Reapers?</u>

Alexander the third of Macedon, or more commonly known as "Alexander the Great" was a Greek King born in the year 356 BC. He inherited the throne of Greece from his father, King Phillip the Second, when he was a mere twenty years old.

His father, King Phillip had been reported as making the claim to Alexander on his death bed, that he thought that the Kingdom that he was leaving for Alexander to preside over, was too insignificant for his character and as such, he encouraged the young Alexander to expand his conquests and Kingdom beyond that which he was about to inherit.

This was something that the young Alexander not only heeded, but also seemed to relish in at the prospect. Considering that his military career had begun even earlier than his inheritance to the throne, as at the age of just sixteen years old, in his father's war against Byzantion, he crushed a Thracian revolt in Macedonia, expelling all the followers of Byzantion, creating a Greek colony, which he then named Alexandropolis.

Having studied under the great Aristotle, Alexander had been made aware of the outer kingdoms in this world, therefore, when he eventually inherited the throne, it was not surprising that Alexander had wished to not only visit the most far-reaching points of the world, but also that he wished to expand his kingdom to the same extent. In 334 BC, Alexander waged war against King Darius of Persia and subsequently crushed Darius's armies. His war with King Darius would ultimately continue until 330 BC, in where

Alexander would claim the throne as the King of Persia.

Alexander was clearly an intelligent young man; however, he was also set on what seemed like, a never-ending campaign to expand his empire as far as he could possibly fathom. In his relatively short reign on the throne, Alexander had managed to conquer and claim rule over all of Ancient Greece, as well as holding the titles such as The Pharaoh of Egypt, the King of Persia, and the Lord of Asia.

During the span of his times of conquest, he had overthrown the lands in which he would ultimately rule over, by way of force and wars, brutally slaying his enemies of the lands he invaded, leaving a mass of death and destruction in his wake. His lust for the claiming of new lands could not last forever, although his success had led him to believe that his armies were invincible. Alexander continued to take what was a tired and exhausted army into Babylon, to which it was reported that Alexander, after a night of drinking, had developed a fever. Although there were rumours that he had in fact been poisoned, although this was never confirmed. At the age of thirty-two, Alexander died in somewhat mysterious circumstances, at the palace of Nebuchadnezzar II in Babylon in June of 323 BC.

In all of Alexander's wars, it has been claimed that he had never lost a single battle. His self-belief was reportedly rivalled only by his seemingly impulsive and reckless demeanour. It has been stated by historians that Alexander often downplayed the achievements of his companions, as well as those of his own father. Often seen upon as narcissistic, Alexander would defy military advice out of a sense of self-indulgent stubbornness.

Despite the mass amounts of death that Alexander left in his wake, he is seen by historians as one of the greatest and most influential people of all time, with some military leaders still using his tactics to this day. Yet, despite the death toll that Alexander had left behind him, his negative traits are often overlooked owing to his success as a leader and conqueror of new lands. Therefore, it potentially raises the question as to whether his narcissistic, stubborn, and seemingly reckless traits would have been shown in such a positive light were he not in the revered position of King of all of these lands.

If he had been from humble backgrounds, trying to expand his fortune by way of claiming small lands by the means of death and individual battle, would he still have been revered in even remotely the same manner?

The characteristics of a person who has been seen to claim a single life is very seldom looked at in any form of a positive outlook. Not that the claiming of any amount of lives should ever be seen as a positive aspect, however, there seems to be somewhat of an ambiguous overtone when the claiming of a life, or in other cases "lives", is differentiated by class or public standing.

In my interviews with Nicolas Claux, the "Vampire of Paris" for my account of his life in my book *Lord of the Dead*, we had many discussions on the concept of how people identify with a person after they have been seen to have been convicted of taking a human life. In our discussions, there is one statement that he made to me, which I think is not only valid, but also sums up the way in which a large number of people think or perceive murder. His statement "If you kill one person you are seen as a monster, but if you kill thousands, you are seen as a conqueror". Quite a potentially controversial statement I will concede, however, the basis for his statement is not one that is without merit.

Throughout recent history, our television documentaries and newspaper reports have been littered with stories of people who have killed another human being in a fit of rage, or by accidental self-defence, or even by nothing short of sheer malice. In the United Kingdom we have had countless reports on people such as Ian Brady with regards to the Moors murders in the 1960's, we have had the murder of the toddler James Bulger in Liverpool in 1993 by Jon Venables and Robert Thompson, as well as the Soham Killings of Jessica Chapman and Holly Wells by Ian Huntley in August of 2002. Whereas in the United States, we have of course, the numerous killings by Ted Bundy in the 1970's, Nicole Brown-Simpson and Ron

Goldman in 1994, in where O.J Simpson had been tried and acquitted of these crimes, as well as the Tate/LaBianca murders in the late 1960's, which the suggested cult known as the "Manson Family" were tried and convicted of having committed.

However, in the same span of approximately fifty years, if you take into account the actions of both the United States Government and that of the United Kingdom, in terms of wars that both of these nations have been involved in, we have the Vietnam War, the Cold War, the Bosnian War, both the first and second Gulf Wars, as well as the invasion of Afghanistan in between the first and second Gulf War. If you take the subsequent death toll of all of these wars combined, the number stands at approximately eight hundred thousand lives that were lost in both civilian and military casualties.

In comparison, when you consider the death toll in both the United States and the United Kingdom for all of the murders that were committed by the perpetrators that have been listed above, the death count stands at approximately forty-nine victims in total. There is a stark contrast to the amount of people that have been killed as the result of military conflict and those whose lives were taken at the hands of convicted murderers. In a perfect world, ideally the numbers calculated from either set of comparison would ideally have been set and remained at zero. However, considering that this is not the case, it gives prevalence that an argument has a basis for being investigated.

From the views expressed in the comparative media and tabloids in both of these countries, in relation to the murders committed by individuals or small groups, the perpetrators of these crimes have been painted in the press as being nothing short of crimes committed by "monsters". Given the way that some of these crimes had been carried out, it would not be an unfair assessment given the nature and brutality of the individual crimes. For the vast majority of the convicted killers, the sentences that were imposed as a result of the convictions seemed relevant and adequate in a lot of people's opinions. However, that does not mean that the victims of death in relation to the relative wars, did not die in any less of a brutal and sadistic fashion. It has been reported that over the years, the weapons of war have been developed in such a manner as to increase the humanitarian fashion that death is delivered to the enemy. Regardless of this, the people have still been killed, no matter what way the manner of death has been delivered. Not to mention that a great number of the deaths associated with these wars, have been civilian casualties as well.

Following the end of the Second World War, there had been many an inquest and subsequent trials pertaining to "War Crimes" that were held to those surviving generals and leaders of Nazi Germany, often leading to the execution or imprisonment of those deemed to have been responsible for the atrocities of the war. Given the information that was displayed to the world in terms of the death camps and persecution of the Jewish people at the hands of the ideals of one man, Adolf Hitler, the resulting fallout of the apprehension of his ringleaders was hardly surprising.

It raises the question as to why the crimes of political leaders, with the exception of Adolf Hitler, are not seen in the same horrific light as those which have been carried out by "monsters" such as cult leaders and serial murderers? One explanation could be that, as much as Adolf Hitler was seen as the face of extreme evil, so were the faces of the cult leaders and serial murderers such as Charles Manson and Ted Bundy. It could be a case of fitting a face to the name of a criminal, in which the public were allowed to gaze upon, as to just who holds the true aspects of evil in the world, just as the case was with Adolf Hitler. As these images of these evils were leaked to the public, the public were able rest comfortably in the safety of their own homes, knowing that such an evil was not in the vicinity of the safety of their own homes, therefore, creating a form of blanket comfort that these evils did not belong to a world in where they conducted their everyday lives.

Another explanation could be that, with the role of recent media, the wars that were being fought on faraway lands, were not portrayed by the media within their own countries as anything other than great leaders who were fighting the evils of another land, not in which to conquer, but to liberate said countries from the hands of their oppressive regimes, in order to bring peace and democracy to a faraway land that was in obvious desperate need for both? Although the world has become a smaller place in terms of connection as a result of the internet and faster communication, with information being far easier to attain that it perhaps would have been thirty or forty years ago, does that mean that the information that we have been drip fed to us is any less biased on the internet than it would be by ways of our local news reports?

Another reason that we do not make the two scenarios of death as a result of international conflict and that of serial murder as comparative is that when the victims of serial crimes are given to us by way of documentaries or news reports, there is far more emphasis given as to who the person is or was, providing the public with accounts and interviews given by the victim's families, as well as providing a form of victimology by way of providing historical details into the victim's history, character, and personality. This is something that we are never given to us by way of detailed accounts in terms of war. We do not get given the lists of people who have died, being either from a military background or civilian, in where age, public standing or even pictures of the deceased people's faces in which to create any form of identity or connection with. The solitary thing that we are provided in terms of war casualties are pictures of the area that has been occupied or the statistics relating to a particular battle as such. The only time that we are shown in times of war, just who from the opposing forces has been captured or killed, is when it is a high-profile leader who has been portrayed as a symbol of modern evils, such as Osama Bin Laden or Saddam Hussein for example. Thus, keeping in line the capture or assassination of someone who has been deemed to us as a "monster" of sorts.

That is not to say that people such as these, are not guilty of atrocities in their homeland, or even harboured the desires to bring destruction in the form of terrorism to our homelands, however, it would be remis of us to not try and understand that our leaders could be being portrayed in similar fashion in the opposing countries of origin.

Our elected leaders try and instil trust and our best interests at heart in their exploits, however, that does not mean that the information that we are being given is the full picture. It is important to remember that both Ted Bundy and John Wayne Gacy were at one point, both interested in politics, only to have had those very aspirations placed to the side of their interest when they were not able to control their desires in which to commit murder. Should they not have indulged in the crimes for which they were eventually convicted, then it is entirely plausible to suggest that they could have rose to similar positions in the future as the very same leaders who sent troops out to wars which resulted in the deaths of thousands.

Politics is not a field which has been without scrutiny, scandal, and even sexual deviance in the past. In fact, there are examples of politicians who have displayed the very Antisocial Personality tendencies as the very "monsters" which have been convicted and imprisoned. Politicians who have shown as little remorse for the people of the lands in which the wars have been fought, with a goal for conquest that could even be deemed as having narcissistic traits. With some members of high-powered world leader positions seeming to have abandoned their grace in a manner which, potentially could be seen as a democratic form of psychopathy. Not to mention other leaders who have indulged in their own reckless sexual deviancy at a time in where they should have been taking care of their respective countries interests instead.

It is difficult to pin point exactly why there would be such significant versions of how differently we look at the exploits of an individual who is responsible for the demise of another. History does not take into account the personal attributes of those of a conquered land in the same manner as a serial murderer. If someone such as "Jack the Ripper" had killed foreign spies as a means to counter espionage as opposed to the murder of prostitutes, then he would have been seen in history as a completely different character entirely.

Historians have the ability to determine how future generations get to perceive murder, whether it be on a mass scale or individual killings. If a world leader was portrayed as having committed genocide, such as the case with Idi Amin, the former President of Uganda, then the killings by someone such as Dr Harold Shipman for example, is bleak in comparison. To which there is the potential for debate as to who the greater "monster" was in retrospect. Which begs the follow-on questions, such as... Is there any difference from our elected officials when compared to others? Were there any signs that our world leaders were able to show remorse? I will leave those questions there for the reader to determine those answers for themselves.

<u>Charles Manson</u>

<u>Born to lead or designed to kill?</u>

The story of the Pied Piper of Hamelin, Germany, is a tale which dates back to times as long ago as the Middle Ages in history. It is a tale of deception, revenge, and in a manner of speaking, compliance as well. However, a startling observation of the story is that of a person who had the ability to lead as well. The story has been told over the ages by people such as Wolfgang von Goethe, The Brothers Grimm, Robert Browning, as well as many others.

In the German town of Hamelin, the town had been savaged by the Plague. The town had an infestation of rats, rats which the locals feared that would spread the "black death" epidemic in quick fashion, creating the fear that the epidemic would have disastrous consequences for the people who inhabited the town. The people of the town had learned that the Pied Piper had the ability in which to play a tune on his pipe, which would draw the attention of the rats and as such, would follow him as he continued to play the tune on his pipes.

The piper was hired by the people of the town to draw the rats away from their homes and as such, save the town's people from the dangers of the ever growing epidemic. The piper did just that, he played his tune and in no time at all, the rats that had infested the German town had all followed him in suit. The piper led the following rats out from the boundaries of the town and once the rats were far enough away from the outskirts, the piper led the rats to a river, in where they all drowned, thus, saving the people of the town from the spread of the deadly plague.

When the piper returned to the town to collect payment for his services, as delighted as they were to be free of rats, they decided that they were not going to pay the piper the money that he was owed. The piper was clearly furious at this turn of events and as such, he warned the town's people that should they not pay him what he was owed, then he would lure the children of the town's inhabitants away from their homes, much in the same fashion as he had done with the plague spreading rats.

The people did not heed the warnings or subsequent threats from the angered piper. As a result, they held fast in their decision not to pay the pied piper. The piper was true to his word. One day a tune could be heard echoing through the streets of the town, it was the piper. He was playing his tune and not before long, the children of the town began to follow the piper and his tune and as a result, left the town in suit. The parents of the children began to plead with the piper to release the children of the town from their trance like following, going as far as to agree to pay the piper the monies that they had initially agreed to. However, it was too late, the piper was no longer interested in receiving the monies that he was owed, instead he remained fixated on exacting his revenge on the people of the town. In fact, it was rumoured that the children were never seen again.

There are several adaptations of this story, one being that all but three children were left behind, one who could not walk in which to follow the piper, one who could not hear the piper's tune, and another who could not see and therefore could not see as where to follow. Another adaptation is told in where the piper returned the children after the people of the town had agreed to pay gold in sums of value far more than was initially agreed for the removal of the rats.

There are morals that can be taken from the story of the Pied Piper in terms of metaphors. Whether it be in relation to sticking to what you have agreed to, being careful of who you invite in to assist you, or the one that I find most useful, being that it is important to heed warnings when they are presented to you.

There are few books relating to a summary of true crime events that would be complete without the inclusion of the infamous Charles Manson. Charles Manson is for a great deal many people, considered to be somewhat of a "bogeyman" in terms of historic murders and criminal events. It covers the topics of drug use, prison life, death penalties, as well as murder. Although it is my understanding that Charles Manson is not considered to be a Serial Killer by a great deal of True Crime enthusiasts, owing to the fact that he never carried out the murders by his own hand.

If we look at the life of Charles Manson, he was born into impoverished conditions to sixteen-year-old Kathleen Manson-Bower-Cavender (Née Maddox) on the 12th of November 1934 in Cincinnati. Such was the manner of Charles Manson having been an unwanted child, it is rumoured that initially Charles Manson was named "No name Maddox". With Manson's biological father having left once he heard of the pregnancy. Prior to the birth, his mother married William Eugene Manson, giving the hope for a possible semblance of a stable family life.

This was not to last, as Manson's mother would opt for drinking sessions with her brother, leaving the young Charles Manson in the care of multiple babysitters, as opposed to being dedicated to the care of her young son. Manson's mother's marriage did not last long and as a result, Charles Manson's stepfather soon opted for divorce. Shortly afterwards, Manson's mother was sent to prison for the charge of assault and robbery, thus, leaving the young Charles Manson to subsequently being placed in the care of his aunt. Following his mother's release from prison, the young Charles Manson was reunited with his mother, however, despite Charles Manson describing these times as what he considered to be "happy times", there is evidence to suggest that his mother opted for a life of drinking and crime, as well as marriage to a man whom she had met through this lifestyle, as opposed to concentrating on raising her young son.

As a result, Charles Manson would begin to falter at school, often playing truant as well as being caught for offences such as theft. At the age of nine, it has been reported that Charles Manson set his school on fire. Despite the requirement of these events being that Manson should have been placed into foster care, there were seemingly no available homes for which he could have been paced into, therefore, as a result, Manson was placed into an institution run by Catholic Priests called the "Gibault School for Boys".

The Gibault school was deemed to be strict, and it was not long before Manson fled the school and returned home to his mother, after having become dissatisfied with the apparent beatings which he had reportedly received. His mother subsequently returned him to the Gibault school for boys, although after a mere ten months, Manson fled once again, only this time he ran away to Indianapolis.

Manson tried his hand at gaining work in which to support himself, although it was not long before he had begun to engage in theft, to which he was apprehended and subsequently sent to a juvenile facility in Omaha, Nebraska. According to his own testimony, Manson was involved in a fight which left a fellow student with a broken arm, thus spearheading his desire for escape, to which he returned to a life of crime as a means to support himself. With the assistance of another one of his fellow students at the facility, they stole a car and used it to assist them in robberies.

Manson was once again apprehended, although this time he was not sent to a facility for boys, but instead he was sent to a strict reform school. A place in which he was reportedly raped by other young inmates, with the encouragement of the staff of the reform school. It is from these attacks in where Manson developed a defence mechanism in where he would flail his arms, screech loudly and give off the impression that he was insane as a means to ward off potential attacks.

After some time, Manson escaped from the reform school, continuing his life of crime as a means to support himself, although he was always eventually apprehended. Each crime that he would commit, would add to his criminal history, thus, giving him the reputation and diagnosis by the experts of the correctional facilities as being of an Antisocial Personality Disorder, with aggressive tendencies.

In the times that Manson was free of correctional facilities owing to his escape, he would continue to engage in criminal activity, even going as far as to drive a stolen car across state lines, which was deemed to have been his first Federal offence. His behaviour would lead from his incarceration in minimum security facilities to eventually being upgraded to a maximum-security unit. Manson would spend the remaining years incarcerated in facilities such as these unto the time of his twenty first birthday, to which he was subsequently released.

Charles Manson made an attempt at having a normal life, he had even become married to Rosalie Jane Willis, to which they had a son whom they named "Charles Manson Jr". However, the wedded bliss of family life would not last long, with Manson having seemingly once again stolen a car and travelled across State lines again. This led to yet another term of imprisonment, which ultimately led to the decline and dissolution of his brief marriage.

Following his parole and despite yet another marriage, this time to a woman named

"Leona", Manson was not about to give up on his life of crime. His criminal activities were comprised of the cashing of forged cheques, as well as even having become involved in the business of prostitution. It was not long before Charles Manson was to be sent back to prison once again, as the inclination towards a life of crime was not one that he was able to refrain from. However, prior to his second term in a maximum-security prison, Manson had become a father for the second time, his second wife having given birth to a son, who was named "Charles Luther". The name of Luther having been the name of his uncle.

At this point, Charles Manson had spent up to half of his life in one form of incarceration or another, whether it had been in the form of juvenile detention facilities, or even maximum-security prisons. Given that Manson has seemingly understood the nature of his own diagnosis, coupled with the fact that he had clearly become institutionalised as a result of having spent so many years in some form of incarceration, it was little surprise that upon the time of his release in 1967, he had actually pleaded with the prison authorities for them to keep him in prison, making the claim that "He couldn't make it on the outside". Naturally, the prison services had no means in where they would uphold Manson's unusual request and as such, he was released back into the free world.

It is during these times in where the story of Charles Manson has been reported to have taken its sinister turn. With the drug fuelled "Hippie" movement of the 60's waning in its positive outlook, only to have been replaced with scenes of street violence and desolation amidst the ever-growing drug culture endemic. There were people who still wished for a cause in which to follow, all the while keeping the focus and positive mindset of "free love", while living a life without boundaries and rules, holding onto the characteristics in which the "hippie" movement was said to represent.

Charles Manson had not experienced much of the hippie movement for himself. For a great portion of the time in where this movement was prevalent, Manson had been in prison. What is more, Manson was slightly older than a great many of the hippies that had wanted to keep the ideals of that time alive. What Manson did have in common with the people of the hippie movement was the common ground of music. Further to this, Manson had developed a skill over the years of having the ability in which to convince people to go along with his plans. Whether it was in juvenile detention facilities in where he would convince fellow inmates to attempt escape with him, or even his second wife, whom he had managed to convince to become involved in the prostitution business. Manson was likeable, more than that, he was believable as being sincere. Therefore, it was not a surprise that with the combination of his pursuit of a musical career, as well as his coercive nature, that so many of the younger generation of hippies seemed to hang on the words and perceptions of Charles Manson.

In what was a relatively short space of time, Manson had gathered a congregation of people who seemed to hang on his words and philosophies as to form something of a collective bubble. The bubble of people gathered in the area of California and comprised of mainly young women, although some males were considered to be a part of the group. People such as Charles "Tex" Watson, Mary Brunner, Susan Atkins, Linda Kasabian, Patricia Krenwinkel, and Leslie Van Houten. The group had dubbed themselves as "The Family", although the press and media would later come to understand the collective for the group as all being members of "The Manson Family".

The "Family" lived at places that were somewhat remote in terms of suburban settlement. Living in the outskirts of towns gave the "Family" the freedom in which to engage in the manner of lifestyle which was non-conformist in terms of modern living. They lived in their ideals of free choice in terms of drug use, the ways, and ideals of how they perceived the world, as well as having music as a major factor in their lives. Although it has been later reported that Manson had dictated what types of music and which bands the "Family" were permitted to listen to. Further to this and especially while living at the Spahn Ranch (a former movie set which was privately owned, yet somewhat dilapidated) in Los Angeles, California, the group practised the ideals of communal living, all the while living their lives according to the teachings of Charles Manson.

At Spahn Ranch, ideology was discussed, all according to the future as Charles Manson had seen it unfolding. In where Manson believed that a Race War was imminent, following which Manson believed that Black People would win the "said war", only that they would not have the capacity in which to rule the country, to which Manson believed would the opportunistic time for his own "Family" to seize control and live out their lives in the manner which they had seen as suitable.

Manson has been portrayed in the testimonies of his followers as being somewhat of a dynamic character, his teachings on what would have been seen by others, as ludicrous statements with regards to things such as religion and politics, as well as unrealistic expectations of his own musical career. Given that Manson had supplied vast amounts of the mind-altering drug LSD to his followers on many occasions, it was not surprising that his teachings were followed almost as a form of gospel. Manson drew inspiration from the musical group **The Beatles**, in particular, the bands **White Album**. Which by the term "Helter Skelter" Manson was able to conjure up his prophetic visions of the imminent "Race War". It was the use of the lyrics of these songs in where Manson was able to not only convince his followers of what was to follow, but also to have them become prepared for such events.

The events that were to follow, which would have been done as a manner in which to begin the "Race War", Manson denies any forms of responsibility for the actions of the "Family". He maintained that each member of the "Family" was acting out of their own free will and that the only thing that Manson himself would have encouraged, was that "if they were going to do something, then do it right". The things that can be referred to as being done "right" were of course what we now know to have been the Tate/LaBianca Murders. In where Sharon Tate, who was not only an actress at the time, but was also the wife of film producer Roman Polanski, along with five other people who were in the Tate/Polanski home on the night, were murdered by the "Manson Family". Not to mention that the actress Sharon Tate was also pregnant at the time of her murder.

In addition to the murders at the Tate/Polanski household, another two murders were committed by the "Family" at the home of the LaBianca's the night following the murders of Sharon Tate and her group of friends. The LaBianca family were a normal, but considerably well-off couple, who the husband Leno, was the Corporate Executive of the State Wholesale Executive Company. Though both the Tate/Polanski and the LaBianca households were considered wealthy, there was little else in which to connect the two sets of murders, leading investigators to not being able to initially connect the opposing murders.

On both crime scenes, there was evidence of excess brutality and disregard for human life, as well as expletives such as "Pig" and the words of "Helter Skelter" supposedly creating the connection for a racially aggravated attack as being the motive for the killings. However, alternate theories suggest that the house in which the Tate murders took place had been previously occupied by Terry Melcher, who was the son of Doris Day, who was a record producer. Although Manson had visited with Melcher at the time he had resided in the house, he had rejected Charles Manson's music by not offering him a record deal following a prior meeting. Therefore, an alternate theory was not that the killings were intended as the catalyst for a "Race War", but instead the occupants of the house at the time of the murders could have been deemed as a form of vicarious revenge against Melcher for the rejection and destruction of Manson's musical career.

Despite Charles Manson having not participated in any of the murders, it has been said that Manson was unhappy at the manner and delivery in which the killings at the Tate/Polanski house had been done. Therefore, as a means to ensure that the next set of killings were conducted to his satisfaction, Manson travelled in the car the following night, to the LaBianca household, so that the next set of killings were "done right". Although Manson disputes this claim.

There are of course, far more details pertaining to both the history of the Manson Family, as well as the killings themselves. However, when the relative "Family Members" were finally arrested, charged, and subsequently convicted of the murders, Manson has always denied his involvement, maintaining his innocence and as a result, maintaining that he has nothing in which to feel remorseful of. It is true that Manson did not commit any of the murders in the physical sense, however, it has been suggested that Manson had coerced his "Family Members" to carry out the killings, another claim in which Manson strenuously denies.

There is little to suggest that Manson has ever shown any signs of not only an admission of any form of guilt, but also that he was ever going to display any forms of emotion or remorse to the killings, in any format. The coercive characteristics seem to fit with Manson's initial diagnosis of his Antisocial Personality Disorder, as does the seeming lack of remorse, regardless of what level he was actually involved in with relation to the killings.

The aspects which make the Manson case difficult to break down, is the fact that from an early age, Manson had spent the vast majority of his time in one form of incarceration or another. So, when the death penalty was removed from Manson's sentence owing to the fact that this particular form of sentence had become temporarily abolished in the United States soon after, there was little hope of prison as a deterrent, nor the hope for rehabilitation owing to the understanding that Manson, by this stage in his life, had become completely institutionalised.

Interviews with Charles Manson, with people such as Diane Sawyer, give rise to the fact that Charles Manson appears to be insane when being filmed. A potential reverting of character back to his earlier years of incarceration, as a self-defence tactic, as to ward off attacks, even though the only person that Manson could be viewing as a potential attacker, would be the people who were interviewing him at the point in time.

It is clear to many that the devolution of Manson's character is a result of not only being let down in terms of a significant role model by his young, yet deviant mother, but also from the very institutions that were supposed to care for him, give him stability, as well as rehabilitate him in his youth. It seems that Charles Manson became nothing more than just a statistic that fell through the gaps, going unnoticed until such a time that his devolution gathered enough gravity, that his antics were implicated in something as sinister as the Tate- LaBianca murders.

Despite documentaries showing that Charles Manson could show moments of lucidity, for example at the times of his parole hearings. Not to mention when you see footage of the moments both post and prior to the interviews with Diane Sawyer, in where Manson was pleasant, friendly, as well as lucid, before transforming both to and from, his defence minded character of acting insane, as well as making inane comments disguised as ludicrous riddles.

The defence character of being insane, as well as his criminal activity, not to mention his reliant on criminal activity, could all be deemed as learned behaviour. Therefore, considering that Manson had been evaluated as having an IQ of 109, despite his apparent illiteracy, it could be argued that these behaviours which led to his devolution, could also be unlearned? There is clear scope for any persons who had the ability to delve into the cognitive workings of Charles Manson, could assist in creating the understanding within Manson that his actions were wrong? Thus, even providing the slight potential that he could not only understand the error of his ways but lead to the possibility that he could understand and potentially feel remorse for what had happened.

I appreciate that such a statement is merely speculative, especially when considering that Manson has since passed away. However, it may give people something to look out for when they search for his interviews and documentaries on his life, with perhaps even a fresh way of taking in the words of Manson himself. Maybe he was the "bogeyman" that he had been perceived to have been, or maybe he was overlooked and misunderstood. It is something that certainly has the potential to raise new questions if we are willing to open up not only our eyes and ears, but also our minds.

Manson could certainly have been seen as a form of Pied Piper. However, the warning signs were all there if only someone had paid attention. Not to mention that we have to look at just who taught him his only tune in which he knew how to play.

<u>Compartmentalisation.</u>

<u>Double life or just lies?</u>

There are very few people in the western world who have not heard of Ian Fleming's James Bond character. While I accept that a vast number of younger people may not be aware of the books from which they originated, almost everyone has heard of the 007 movies which have been spring-boarded onto the silver screen.

The screen adaptations of Ian Fleming's books have been influential in boosting the careers of people such as Roger Moore, Pierce Brosnan, Daniel Craig, as well as the revered Sean Connery. Each one of these actors have provided their own twists on the James Bond character, however, they all maintain the one fundamental purpose of what James Bond is truly about, that being of espionage.

The lure of a spy-based movie has always been a subject of intrigue, especially in the case of James Bond movies. We are often left on the edge of our seats, wondering where the next nail-biting twist is going to come from. The fact that the silver screen "hero" of James Bond is often forced into transforming himself into various deceptive roles or false characters in order to gain the trust of a would-be villain, so that he is able to "save the world", in a scenario that the viewer often relishes.

The glamour of the expensive Austin Martin cars, as well as being accompanied by women who are often potential "Miss World" candidates, is a lifestyle that has left many a person watching the movies in a fit of jealousy. However, the same cannot be said for the death-defying antics and dangerous encounters that seem to balance the pros and cons of the espionage lifestyle.

It can be said that when James Bond is back at MI6, the headquarters in London that deals with matters of international significance, that he is shown to display his true character, that being a character of lesser arrogance and more akin to a dutiful civil servant, albeit with a licence to kill.

So, what is it about his international exploits that makes James Bond able to switch from his mindset of a dutiful civil servant, to that of a danger fraught, international man of mystery? The intrigue into Bond's character stems in part, from the fact that he is able to switch seamlessly from one character to another with the utmost of ease. Characters who are determined to save the world at all costs.

What makes this transformation so awe-inspiring is the fact that his ability to turn from character to character, from mindset to mindset, without ever letting a single portion of his life transcend into the other, is that the well-trained Spy James Bond is able to compartmentalise. However, as Bond is doing this for the purposes of saving mankind, there is little to deflect from his transformations in a mental focus. Now imagine that this was not the case, that the purposes and intent of the character was doing so for their own ends, consistent with evil and malevolence. Imagine for example, the same ability to compartmentalise, but with a serial killer...

There are many aspects of life in which we compartmentalise, therefore, it is not just at the sole application of fictional book or movie characters and that of serial killers. People compartmentalise in their everyday lives. Quite often a person could be described in the work place as being "different in work compared to outside of work". That is because when we are at work, we are there to do a job and as such, being professional quite often means that we are encouraged to leave things such as emotion out of our everyday working decisions. For example, a person who works for a debt collection agency. They are employed for the sole reason of the collection of monies that are either owed to them, or their company that has been employed to recover the indebted funds of a third-party company, which do not have the resources in which to debt-collect efficiently.

The person who has been given a single debt case in which to collect the funds, is then charged with the duty of using whatever means they have at their disposal to collect the relevant monies. The person then telephones the person who owes the company money, only to be told that they do not have the means in which to repay the debt. Potentially the conversation then takes a turn for the worse, with the person on the receiving end of the phone call in apparent tears as they are having financial difficulties and are unable to repay the money that is owed. The debt collector is seemingly unmoved and as such, informs the tear-stricken person in financial difficulty that they have no option other than to refer the matter to a civil court, with the potential for the courts removing their assets unless the debt is to be paid back in full.

That does not mean that the person who has been placed in charge of recovering the money from the tear-stricken party does not have any sympathy for their situation, however, as they are to act professionally, they cannot allow themselves to show any forms of weakness or an unrelenting stance. As it means that the debt collector could be chastised for not doing their job properly. Privately and in their mind, there is the very real probability that the person who is charged with collecting the debt does hold sympathy for their tear-stricken counterpart, however, if they were to allow this sympathy to show, then there is every chance that they would be inefficient in doing their job. Increasing the possibility of being marked down in their company's performance evaluations.

Following several telephone conversations of similar ilk throughout their working day, the debt collector finally finishes work and leaves for home for the day. There may be a few lingering thoughts as to some of the phone conversations that they have had throughout the day, however, once they are away from the workplace, these thoughts become nothing more than potential statistics, as they are now focussed on their own personal lives.

The point in this is that the debt collector has played nothing more than a role in their place of work. They view it as just "what they do" as opposed to "who they are". It may be seen as deceitful in the fact that they are playing a role of a debt collector that has no sympathy towards their debt-laden counterparts, however, as they are essentially playing a professional role so that they can earn a living themselves, they are able to compartmentalise what they do in their professional life. Therefore, enabling them to live in the manner they wish to in their private lives.

If we take the same view towards soldiers of any country, who have been employed by the government, to not only defend our lands from foreign attack, or as is with the case in more recent times, when soldiers have been deployed to another country in the fight for worldwide democracy.

A soldier will have been trained to military standards and then deployed to a place such as Iraq for example. Whilst in Iraq, the soldier will most likely have to face situations in where armed combat is not only something which they have been trained for, but also something that is to be expected. As I understand it, both British and United States military forces leave their homelands for specific amounts of time, known as "tours", of the foreign places of conflict.

Whilst in these conflict zones, as is the case with many a war zone, there are large scale numbers of deaths as a result of military operations. The Soldier has to quite often, shoot the enemy, or deploy missiles, or even in the case of military medics, attend to the wounded or dead following the outbreak of a specific conflict. With the exception of the medics in this case, the soldiers have been trained to kill, with the consideration that their enemies have not surrendered at the

first point of a skirmish, then that is exactly
what they will have done. This is nothing at
all to suggest that any form of negativity is
being pointed in the direction of any person
who is serving their country. Quite the
contrary, as despite anyone disagreeing with
the reasons for any particular war, that
should not deflect that the soldiers who have
been ordered into battle are not anything
short of courageous. However, the simple
fact of this point is that these soldiers will
have been forced to have taken the lives of
their enemies at certain stages in their
military careers.

Following the "tour" of the respective lands
of which they are fighting in, the soldiers
then are returned home for a period of time,
where they get to spend time with their
loved ones, get time to relax and recuperate,
as well as get a welcomed return to a "normal
life" for a period of time, before they are
called upon for their next assignment. While

I fully appreciate that some of the soldiers who are returning from conflict zones find it difficult to make that transition back to "normal life" after having served in a conflict zone, there are also a vast amount of people who can make that transition back to "normality" with relative ease. In where they are able to show love to their families.

In their "normal" lives, it should be understood that these soldiers are quite often normal people. People who, like the rest of us, make mistakes, have arguments with their loved ones and sometimes, break the law and have to go to court for their actions. As with arguments and crimes, it is often that we are able to admit guilt, show remorse for our behaviours and our actions, as well as doing things to rectify our behaviours. A great deal of soldiers who have returned home are no different in that respect. They are able to show humility, love, and even remorse. However, when it comes to the actions that they have been ordered to undertake in times of war, there is quite often the case that there is little, to no emotion being shown in terms of what they have been ordered to do, as it is part of their professional military careers.

In the book by Michaud and Aynesworth, ***Ted Bundy: Conversations with a killer***. Ted Bundy makes the reference to soldiers in wars such as Vietnam, in where he speaks about soldiers who have been in places of war, killing under orders and as such, not suffering from the emotional effects of their killings in these wars. His reasons for such an observation being that, in war times, the enemy was quite often deemed as being faceless and without personality. Quite often soldiers have described their enemies in such a manner as to almost dehumanise them as people, for the purposes of making it easier in which to eliminate the enemy. By doing so, it has mentally created that separation from the lives that they were taking in war, from the lives of the people that are in their own world. Creating a clear distinction in their minds between their own lives and the lives of the opposition, so that they were able to carry out the killings that they have been ordered to do.

The soldiers which Bundy referred to, would then be able to return home, live their lives with all of their human emotions in tact to a degree. Allowing emotions such as love, remorse, happiness etc, to remain as a prevalent factor in their post-war lives. This dehumanisation of their enemy is nothing short of being a manner in which to compartmentalise their actions during times of war. Done in this manner so that they could places their deeds of war in something of a "mental box" and then carry on with their regular lives as best that they could.

It is not just in the lives and minds of soldiers and debt collectors that such a mental facility is allowed to remain active. Many professions, such as Paramedics, Firefighters, Hospital Nurses and Doctors, as well as Police Officers, all have to deal with tragedy and death on a daily basis, having to witness horrific sights in their daily lives, yet for the purposes of maintaining a healthy and productive family and personal life, they are forced to compartmentalise the sights and events of their professional lives, so that they can display the very emotions that have been listed in the previous paragraph. That does not mean that those emotions are non-existent in their lives, it is just that they have been compartmentalised for what could be argued as "the greater good" in the other aspects of their lives as a whole.

In the case of Serial Killers, it is quite often claimed that due to disorders such as an Antisocial Personality Disorder, it is highly likely that a Serial Killer diagnosed with such a disorder is not able to understand or even feel, emotions such as guilt or even remorse. However, there have been cases of killers who have been arguably the most difficult in which to apprehend, that they were able to conduct their daily lives outside of their murder sprees in such a fashion that they were not identified as people who would have had the capacity to kill.

It is accepted that a Serial Killer who has been giving such a diagnosis is often said to be a person that is not only manipulative, but also coercive and devious at the same time. Having said that, another trait which is commonly connected to a Serial Killer of such a diagnosis could be seen to displaying traits of recklessness, as well as a high degree of narcissism. Owing to the fact that killers such a Ted Bundy and even Jack the Ripper, were able to conduct their murderous activities in a fashion, in where Ted Bundy for example, brought with it complete shock as to the fact that he was even capable of being a murderer. Even if you look at the case of Jack the Ripper, while there has been speculation as to just who Jack the Ripper actually was, there has never been any definitive conclusion as to his identity. This leads us to believe that not only was he able to continue his life outside of the killing of the prostitutes that were his victims, but also that he was able to put his murderous lifestyle to one side once he had completed his series of murders.

This gives rise to the potential suggestion that both of these killers were able to compartmentalise their killings so that they did not hinder what would be their everyday lives outside of these acts. Owing to a diagnosis which would have included recklessness and narcissism as key traits, it would have meant that this would not be possible. Yet, when you look at the fact that both Elizabeth Kendall, as well as Carole Boone, the intimate partners, of which the latter became Bundy's wife, in where they were both able to state that at certain points they felt as though Bundy had shown and felt love towards them. Then it brings forward the possibility that the killings that Bundy had done, were done in a manner of compartmentalisation. Bundy was able to not only get on with his everyday life, but in that life show emotion to his partners and subsequently, show remorse for his crimes at a later date. This remorse being spoken of after having finally confessed in full during the run up to his eventual execution.

There is plausibility that a Serial Killer, much in the same manner as a soldier in war, could in their own minds, dehumanise their victims so that they were nothing more to the Serial Killer than faceless beings. If they were to compartmentalise their killings in such a fashion, then there would be no remorse or emotion towards their victims. However, in their day-to-day life, a life shut off in their minds from a world of killing, then they would certainly have the plausibility of showing and displaying emotions such as guilt and remorse for the actions relating to their lives outside of the world of serial murder.

What there is a potential argument against, is that such a serial criminal not being able to feel the emotions of remorse in their entirety. If it was a case of a Serial Killer conducting their activity as a form of compartmentalising, then the blanket diagnosis of Antisocial Personality Disorder given to many a killer is too vague in which to be accurate. Unless the diagnosis is split to determine only the state of mind in where compartmentalisation has taken place. As remorse, guilt, love, and happiness, and all the emotions of a killer that are "not possible", are all quite prevalent in their normal, ordinary, day-to-day life.

There is no argument as to the heinousness of the deeds that have been separated from the rational state of the "boxed off" mind of a Serial Killer. However, in such a case, there is argument against these emotions being lacking, when it is more of a case that for certain aspects of their lives, they have been purposely blocked off, as opposed to not having the ability of "being there" in the first place. Therefore, compartmentalising would lead to us to think that the Antisocial Personality Disorder as a diagnosis, is at best, only partly possible to be completely accurate.

These killers, soldiers, medical professionals, all have the ability to feel and understand emotion. Emotions which include guilt and remorse. It is more likely that these emotions may be void when the process of compartmentalisation has been introduced as a psychological coping strategy.

<u>Criminal Profilers</u>

<u>True Frontline Heroes</u>

The term "Hero" is one that, like so many of our modern-day words, is derived from Greek origins. In ancient Greek mythology, the actual definition of the word "Hero" is actually used when describing a "Dead Man" who had achieved fame in his life and as such, upon his death, his grave transformed as a form of a shrine, to give the deceased person the power in which to either support or protect the living.

The subsequent "Hero" was then viewed, owing to their exploits in life, as being more than the average human. However, they remained at a lesser status than that of a God. Thus, bringing into existence, the demi-god category of human who was deemed worthy of the "Hero" status.

Naturally, there would also have been Gods in which the Ancient Greek people deemed to be of "Hero" status as well, suggesting that the line for distinction between a "Hero" and a "God" becoming somewhat diminished on occasion.

Although in Greek times, the "Hero" was given their status once they had passed on in life, with the shrines that they crafted on the tombs of their fallen idols being created so that they would be protected by their "Hero". The deceased person was given the same fame and adulation in death, as much as they had been perceived to have had in life, with the sole ideals that the deceased person would then support and protect the people, much in the same manner as they were able to whilst they had still been alive.

The key words that seem to have remained akin to the "Hero" throughout the ages seems to be those of support and protect. The modern-day hero is, therefore, a person who seems to replicate these ideals of ancient Greece, all the while applying the words in practice, to whatever the needs and measures that are needed in a modern-day society.

In terms of True Crime, there are many people whose actions can be seen as being worthy of such a status. People such as Medical Staff, all Emergency Services, to even just a passer-by in the street who sees another fellow human in need of assistance, who then risks their own well-being, so that they can help another. All of these people could be deemed as "Heroes". However, there is one type of person that often gets overlooked, that being the hero of the criminal profiler.

Almost all people who are interested in True Crime as a subject, are quite often partial to watching fictional programmes on TV such as that of the extended series "Criminal Minds". This fictional program, whilst being filmed under the common theme of serial murder, amongst various other kinds of crime scenarios, is actually centred upon the lives and professions of the Behavioural Analysis Unit of the FBI in the United States.

In this program, we watch in awe as the members of FBI team, use their knowledge of criminal behavioural patterns in order to apprehend a suspected killer or criminal. Naturally, this is of course a fictional program, one which, according to approval ratings, is of high standard content. However, the idea for such a team of elite crime fighting heroes, is not one that came from that of a fictional imagination. This very type of professional exists in our lives, using their profound knowledge of criminal activity, in order to keep our streets free from dangerous criminals as best possible.

The criminal profiler quite often has to deal with the one type of crime that strikes fear into the hearts of the majority of law-abiding citizens, that being murder. The cases that the "Profiler" has to deal with can often be isolated incidents of murder, however, as it quite often the case, it is the job of the profiler to have to deal with cases pertaining to that of a serial offender, or even a Serial Killer.

This type of profiler is not just a person who has studied Psychology, or even a person who has specialised in Criminal Psychology as such. There is far more to their roles than a mere study of Psychology. The profiler, throughout years of various forms of training and study, will have adapted their learning of psychological traits, combined with their experience in the field of law enforcement, so that they can study cases in order to apprehend a suspected offender. Quite often, there is little to suggest that the person that they have determined to be their person of interest in a particular case, is not the correct suspect, mainly because their analysis of just who it is that they are looking for, leads them to the point of making an arrest based on precision detailing of the behaviours of a suspected offender.

Significantly, the Profiler takes their potential knowledge of the psychology of an offender and combines their findings of details of a crime scene, coupled with things such as victimology and possible signature details in order to establish just what kind of person would be responsible for the crime in which they are investigating. Things such as victimology and signature details are pivotal, in that the learning of the concurrent aspects of a victim can lead the profiler to understand just what groups of people are the most likely to become vulnerable to a potential attack from the offender. What is more, if there are signature details present at the crime scenes, for example, if each victim of an offender were all killed in a similar fashion, it can lead us to understanding that a potential Serial Killer is in fact responsible for the crimes in question.

The lists of details in which the Profiler collates is endless. The manner in which a person, or a number of people have been killed, can tell us a lot about the individual who is carrying out these crimes. For example, if stab wounds were tentative, then it is entirely plausible that the killer showed remorse, or even that they have not fully devolved as yet. If the corpse of a person has been left in a place which is easy to discover, then it is plausible that the killer has done this purposely, in order to make a "statement" as such to the public. Potentially in defiance as to not receiving the attention that the killer may feel that they deserve, or even warrant. A further example of a signature detail would be, a corpse of a victim which has been left in a place which is communal in nature, yet the corpse has been covered once the killer has committed his crime potentially gives rise to the possibility that the killing was done as a matter of impulse, yet once they have satisfied their need to kill, they have felt shame or remorse and covered the corpse so that the killer does not have to face what it is that they have just done.

All of these aspects are taken into consideration by the Profiler, in order to paint a mental picture and character of the person who may be responsible for these crimes. The potential details that have been listed above are just a fraction of the possibilities in which a Profiler would have in order to make a calculated assumption. The significance in this is that the profiler, although using theories of a psychological nature, takes each case on its individual merit, so that they can create a profile which is unique to the possible killer in which they are dealing with at that particular given time. While the Psychological theories which could be seen as generalised in the broader spectrum, are a foundation for the base of their "profiles", it is the application of the specific details of the crimes they are investigating which provide the potential of painting a clearer mental picture of the killer in question.

With the understanding that no one murder case, unless a "copycat" killing, is exactly the same as another. It is vital that the knowledge of the profiler's continuous study of historic cases is taken into consideration, as this allows the profiler to easier understand just what kind of killer they are searching for, before narrowing down their suspect lists by use of individual details pertaining to the relevant crime scenes. This knowledge of historic crimes, not only assists the profiler in catching the killer that they are searching for, but also puts in place the possibility of the prevention of murder, as it is easier to stop a killer from creating a death toll of perhaps thirty victims, if their applied knowledge creates the opportunity to halt the killer before they manage to claim such a high number of lives.

The Profiler that I have found to be the most insightful and dedicated to not only the solving of cases, but also spreading his knowledge of Serial Killers as a means to prevent crimes of this nature, is Robert D Keppel. Keppel is a former Law Enforcement Officer from the State of Washington, who was instrumental in the capture of Ted Bundy. Having initially narrowed down a list to just twenty-five people as suspects in the "Ted Killings", to which Bundy was named as a potential candidate. Further to this, Keppel was recruited to advise on the "Riverman" killings in Seattle, Washington, by way of working with the incarcerated Ted Bundy, in where the collaboration resulted in the working profile of the "Green River Killer", Gary Ridgeway, who was eventually apprehended in November 2001.

Over the course of Keppel's career, he worked on approximately two thousand homicide cases, initially working as a Law Enforcement officer for the King County Sheriff's Department, as well as contributing seventeen years as the Chief Criminal Investigator for the Attorney General's Office of the State of Washington. In addition, working as a consultant to many other cases across the United States, as a means to assist in the apprehension of violent offenders. In addition to his years of service to Law Enforcement, Keppel has also furthered his own studies by obtaining qualifications in

Psychology by way of not only becoming a Doctor of Philosophy in Criminal Justice, but also obtaining a Master of Arts Degree in Police Science. Therefore, Keppel has crossed all spectrums of combining Psychological expertise with his vast amount of experience obtained in his Law Enforcement career, to become one of the most revered and credible focal points of the mindset of not only Serial Killers, but criminals in general.

Further to this, Robert D. Keppel PhD, has written several books relating to is expertise on the subject. To which some of his books have been used as a means of reference in terms of identifying and apprehending violent criminals and Serial Killers. Books which have in essence, become *THE* handbooks for study by the next induction of recruits in Law Enforcement agencies across the world today. In his books, Dr Keppel breaks down the many possible scenarios of how to identify and apprehend a Serial Killer, however, further than that, he teaches the reader or would-be recruit, to also break down the fundamental issues within a particular Law Enforcement agency which could possibly hinder an investigation in its infancy stages. By this, I am referring to things such as ego or stubbornness, all things which often create difficulties when various departments have to swallow their pride and admit that there is a need to work collectively as opposed to individually, but also in as simple a mindset of accepting that certain crimes are related to a serial murderer, dealing with the numbers of victims as a collective whole. Therefore, simplifying their efforts in order to place the focus where it needs to be, on solving the case.

Dr Keppel's work has been instrumental the world over, in solving cases at an earlier stage in developments, therefore, not allowing the potential number of victims to escalate. His knowledge and experience have been pivotal in just how people view the habits and workings of violent criminals and Serial Killers, so that we not only are able to keep such offenders off our streets, but in doing so, save the lives of countless future victims going forward.

In his work, Dr Keppel has not merely based his insight on simple Psychopathy or even Sociopathy. Nor has he simply relied on only his years of law enforcement experience. Details of his reports have showed us that quite often, we are not merely dealing with a Serial Killer as a single entity. The type of Serial Killer has the potential to be as diverse as any other type of person in our societies. Breaking down the Serial Killer to varied different kinds of behavioural patterns, only to then break down those personality types into further sub-divisions, so that the Law Enforcement officer is then able to narrow his scope as to who it is that might be responsible for the crimes. Dr Keppel shows us killers from various potential mental capacities, in that there are those who are of a Psychopathic nature, to those that show remorse, those that are indulgent of sexual gratification but are unable to do so without the requirement for violent behaviour. There are windows into the mindset of killers who commit crimes for as many varied reasons as there are types of victims. Each showing an individual emotional state, often matching with the behaviour related to the crimes that they have committed. In my studies of Dr Keppel's works, it shows me that nothing should ever be ruled out as a possibility, as the ruling out of a potential mindset could be the key to overlooking significant facts in the study of a Serial Killer. With each detail that we see being as significant to understand as the very details that we choose to eliminate.

Dr Keppel is a man who, has combined the studies of the human mind, with his knowledge of his vast and extensive experience in Law Enforcement, so that in a manner of speaking, has collated the worlds of the Old with the New, so that we can live in a more protected world. This protection provides us with the means to support the public in a manner that we are able to live a healthier and safer life.

By the definition of a person who is deemed to be a "Hero", in that the person who has been given this status as being one who is seen to both protect us and support the lives of others, then it is not unfathomable that a man such as Dr Keppel could easily be placed in this category. This man has dedicated his years of experience as well as furthered his intellectual knowledge of the mind of a killer so that we are not only able to remove dangerous people from the streets of the world, but in retrospect, has saved the lives of countless others by way of his unwavering dedication. The world of Law Enforcement would not have the ability to keep us safe in the manner of which we have come to rely on if it were not for people such as Dr Keppel. Therefore, in both the modern and ancient sense of the word, there is no question that this is a person deserving of such a title or accolade. Dr Keppel is a hero by any standards which people wish to measure the word.

In the non-fictional world of True Crime, there is the same comparison to be made between the heroes and villains as there is in the fictional world. Granted that the devious and callous nature of the villain is often what is remembered the most by people, as it is the criminal who the newspapers and media tend to focus on as a means to sell sensationalism. However, it would be remiss to not include the very people that have made it possible for us to have the luxury of being able to sit in our homes and read such stories. The world is a safer place because of such heroes, therefore, their mention in things pertaining to the world of crime is entirely relevant and deserves our acknowledgement.

Sadly, at the time of writing, Dr Robert Keppel passed away after a period of illness. The world of Law Enforcement and Crime prevention will always be grateful for his valued service.

<u>The Workings of the Mind</u>

<u>Degeneration to the point of Redevelopment</u>

Nature is a form of balance. With most things in nature, a depletion of balance is an opportunity for potential chaos and disruption. Without the sense of balance, there is little to suggest the maintenance of any sense of harmony, leaving the probability for a potential recipe for disaster.

A Volcano that lays dormant for many years is nothing short of peaceful at the best of times, however, when the pressure beneath the core of the volcano becomes unbalanced and the subsequent residents of the surrounding areas of the Volcano do not pay heed to the potential warnings, then there is ultimately the potential for destruction to their properties and even lives, should the Volcano erupt and nothing has been done to evacuate prior to the Volcano erupting with clouds of ashes and molten lava.

Even if we simplify the basis for which balance could be viewed, in something as simple as cooking, or baking a cake. The perfect balance of ingredients is vital for the perfect end result of the cake in question. Too much flour in the mix would result in a lack of a fluffy texture, or even forgetting to place sugar into the ingredients bowl would leave the balance of taste to be somewhat wanting in terms of perfection.

The balance is, however, not always lost. Granted that when a cake has been baked with the absence of sugar, there is an alternate means in which to provide the missing sweetness. By way of things such as icing, in which to even the scales for our tastebuds.

Much in the same way that the raging Volcano often becomes dormant once again, following the lava eruption which has the potential to cause damage. The raging volcano restores its own sense of balance, bringing back the sense of tranquillity to an area which it had, prior to the eruption, enjoyed for lengthy periods of time.

Therefore, there is possibility to suggest that the same manner of balance in the human mind, as an element of nature, is not beyond comprehension. Much in the same manner as the pressure of a Volcano can ascend and descend, then the balance of a mind has that same ability to balance the offset chemicals following a time of turmoil and potential destruction.

———————————————

Life brings us many scenarios in where our capability for mental function is subject to change. This is partially due to the chemical balances in our brains, which can often account for not only our emotions, but also in the manner in which we are seen to perceive things.

In my research for the plausibility of the potential for remorse in Serial Killers, I have consulted with a number of different people for opinion and potential for this possibility. In my research, I have spoken to a trusted Psychologist, who will remain nameless due to the fact that this Psychologist runs a family practice and as such, wishes to remain out of the spotlight, owing to the fact that the topic of being connected to serial murder theories could impact upon their practice. What I will say about this Psychologist is that, on a personal level, I have trusted my inner most issues with them, helping to clear the fog of the mind by taking not only a cognitive approach to the issues, but also a humanistic approach as well. Something which I have found to be not only grounding, but fundamentally significant in the road to personal recovery.

In our discussions regarding the plausibility of a Serial Killer being able to feel and show remorse, there were a number of alternate scenarios which gave the potential for cognitive development which could potentially alter the mindset of many people, which could even include those convicted of serial murder.

The first being that, if we take a person who has suffered a Cerebrovascular Accident. (CVA), or as it is commonly known as, a Stroke. This is a condition which is caused by the flow of blood to the brain becoming obstructed, in where a blood clot will obstruct the flow of blood to the brain,

resulting in the aforementioned "Stroke".
Another kind of Stroke is when there is
haemorrhaging of blood to the brain, caused
by weakened blood vessels, which surround
the brain with blood, constricting and
compressing the tissue of the brain, leading
to the Cerebrovascular Accident. The result
of both of these types of Strokes quite often
becomes fatal. However, as is quite often the
case, any persons surviving a stroke, has
impaired body motor function, owing to
damage in the person's brain tissue.

A person who is recovering from a stroke will
often find it difficult to recover from such an
accident, with the loss of speech and motor
function being the two most prevalent
results from such an event. It is a slow and
difficult recovery, but it is not impossible.
Through a series of therapies, quite often a
patient who has suffered a stroke will learn
to rediscover the use of their body and verbal
communication skills, albeit that seldom do

they ever recover to one hundred percent of their ability that was in place prior to the stroke occurring.

The significant factor in this, however, is that there is evidence of neurological recovery. Regardless of the ultimate percentage of just how much the patient is able to recover. Therefore, if we liken this scenario to a person who has been deemed to have committed Serial Murder as a result of Neurological Damage being the main factor in a person's ability to distinguish between right and wrong, or even to have been aware of their manifestations of their crimes or the ability in which to control their actions, then it could be said that, through a series of cognitive therapy, much in the same manner of goals in terms of assisting stroke victims with neurological damage, then why is the plausibility of similar recovery for this type of Serial Killer then also not a possibility?

This is not to suggest that a person with a diminished neurological capacity would ever be "recovered" enough to resume their place within society, however, we can make the same comparison that a stroke victim may never fully regain their full use of motor function and speech capabilities. This is in no way to suggest that the killer suffering from neurological abnormality could one day be set free, however, it does raise the possibility that there is a potential for a degree of cognitive recovery in that the Serial Killer could develop the sense of determining right from wrong, holding a sense of responsibility for their crimes and in turn, placing the suggestion that they could ultimately feel guilt and remorse for their crimes.

It goes without saying that such a probability would be difficult in which to achieve. However, when you look at the person who has suffered a stroke, the time that it can potentially take for a patient to recover to a workable degree in terms of motor and speech function, it is not something that happens overnight. Quite often, it could take months or even years to have gained even a small degree of positive recovery. Therefore, if we are to allow for a similar timescale in terms of neurological recovery for the actions of a Serial Killer, then surely there is a potential for hope for recognition of acknowledgement and emotion in connection to their crimes?

Conditions such as Dementia and Alzheimer's can have devasting effects, for both the patients themselves, as well as for the family of the patients. In both of these diagnoses, there is a deterioration factor which leads to impair the patient's ability in which to function. Quite often there is a significant amount of memory loss, which leads patients who suffer from such a horrific disease to forget not only simple things, as how to locate certain items in their own homes, but also to lose track of where they are at times, forgetting the reasons for being in a particular place, even forgetting on how to find their way home on occasion. Not to mention, the single biggest issue, of not being able to recognise members of their own family or the closest of lifelong friends. These issues can be extremely distressing for people who are unfortunate enough to fall foul to these conditions. Not to mention, the stress and worry that is raised within members of their families who are concerned for the welfare of the person who is suffering with the condition.

The ability of the human brain is something that we have not been able to understand as yet to the full extent of its capacity. Therefore, there are different techniques that are being applied in practice all of the time, which have shown positive results being recorded. A type of cognitive therapy known as Maintenance Cognitive Stimulation Therapy (MCST) has been developed with the early stages of Dementia as a focal point, in where patients partake in cognitive activity within a group surrounding, so that activities such as music, discussions, physical activity, as well as creative activity are all used as a means in which to trigger not only memory, but act as a stimulus in order to maintain the activity of a particular brain function.

The function of MCST has proven to have documented positive results, being one of the few cognitive therapies which have shown to maintain brain function without the use of medication. There are groups called "reminder sessions" which have been implemented in order to trigger memory function, therefore, maintaining positive activity in the brain. This is just one cognitive method which has shown positive results over the years. There have been other

cases recorded in where, a group of
Dementia patients have been sat in a group,
quite often with patients who have had
significant deterioration of the brain, when
all of a sudden, with the trigger of a musical
note, have suddenly remembered a particular
dance and as a result, have raised themselves
from their seated position, in an attempt to
dance to the song which they have
remembered. This being the result of a
neurological trigger which has served to
activate a dormant memory within the
patient.

In the world of Psychology, there is still so
much that we do not know with regards to
the human brain. Granted that there are
visible physical imperfections, which can be
made visible by use of a brain scan, or even
physical examination of the human brain
following a post mortem, all which could
point to neurological factors which could
impair the brain. For example, following the

result of an M.R.I scan, which showed damage to the frontal lobe of the brain, it would indicate that there may be a loss of function with regards to damage of the neurons which control the aspects of personality changes, concentration, and even impulsivity. Should the damage, which is shown on the scan, be irreversible, then it is understood that these changes in personality could also therefore, be irreversible as well.

Should an MRI scan show no subsequent damage to the frontal lobe within the brain (Example Ted Bundy) then there is reason to suggest that such impulsive acts and personality change would not necessarily be irreversible, meaning that the potential for change is a possibility. As with patients who have been diagnosed with Dementia or Alzheimer's, in that there is the possibility to invoke memory by means of a Psychiatric trigger, then there should be enough cause for the probability of a person who is deemed to be a Serial Killer having the possibility of invoking an emotional response such as guilt or emotion, by means of the application of a psychiatric trigger. As part of a potential rehabilitation process, a healthy alternative would be to discover just what that potential psychiatric trigger would be, to then cultivating it for positive results going forward. Implementing a means of Cognitive Therapy to yield positive results. These results not only showing the potential for real human emotion, but also serving to eradicate the impulse to commit murder in the first place.

The reasons for diagnoses for ailments such as depression, anxiety, the ability in which to manage your emotions, is quite often linked by a chemical imbalance in the mind. For example, when there is an increase or decrease in our Serotonin levels, it has the ability in which to influence our moods and emotions for the better or for the worse. It is our ability in which we handle these emotions or words that ultimately determine our resulting actions. If the chemical imbalance has been swayed so significantly to the side of the negative, then the lack of the ability in which to handle these emotions can make a person act irrationally, or even impulsive to the point of severe aggression. Quite often, a person who has committed murder, will say that they could not control their actions, or even state that they felt as though they were not in control of their own minds, leading them to carry out the heinous act of murder, in a ruthless and uncompromising fashion. If these moments of disparity which led the person to such acts were on a regular basis, then we would be dealing with someone who would be deemed to be a Serial Killer.

Now an impulsive act could be deemed as a moment of Psychopathy, however, the understanding of what is happening often accrues when the emotions of a person has released their pent-up impulsive aggression, leaving them with an alternative set of emotions once the murder has been completed. The fear or understanding of potentially being caught for their crimes takes over, resulting in the person covering their tracks and disposing of evidence so that they are not caught for their crime. What is not being addressed by the person, is the cycle in which their emotions are becoming manifested, therefore, their cycle will often continue until someone, or something intervenes. Usually, that would be Law Enforcement.

The chemical imbalance which is causing this turbulence of emotions is something, that if dealt with, by way of therapy or medication coupled with therapy, could be brought to a halt.

It is quite plausible that the mind has encountered something that has resulted in the subsequent chemical imbalance becoming triggered, resulting in the lack of control of the emotions and resulting actions. Therefore, it is suggestable that something can be done in which to not only get to the root of what causes this imbalance to become triggered, but also that this chemical balance has the potential to be restored, resulting in the removal of an impulse to invoke violent behaviours.

A lack of control of the Serial Killer's emotions is not the same thing as these emotions being absent from their mind. It is the inability to balance the emotion within themselves. Therefore, meaning that if the killer has the ability in which to become imbalanced as a result of a chemical composition, then there is the possibility of balance restoration, in which normal emotions such as guilt, remorse, happiness and so forth, can be felt and understood at a level deemed to be normal.

From a psychological point of view, there are many comparisons which could be made from an elderly person who has been placed in a secure unit such as a care home, or mental health facility and a Serial Killer, or serial criminal which has been placed in prison for an extended period of time. Although it may seem controversial to make such a comparison, it is not without merit. Both of which have been placed in their respective facilities so that they are no longer a danger to either themselves or those around them. Both are placed in such a facility so that there is a hope for rehabilitation, whether it be for the physical sense in terms of an elderly patient, or for their behaviours as is the case with certain criminals.

There are countless organisations which are dedicated to the research of patients who are suffering with the ailments of a Dementia or

Alzheimer's diagnosis. Yet, despite there often being little hope of a full recovery from the respective diseases, the search for improvement continues. Despite the view of many that the patient in question is "gone" in terms of mental capacity, the research goes on in the hope of bringing some of the brain function back to the patient.

It would therefore suggest, that in the case for persons who have been convicted of serial murder, that unless there is evidence of permanent damage to the frontal lobe of the brain, in where there is zero hope of recovery, then why it is that more research is not done in terms of understanding the development within the mind of a killer? There is enough evidence to suggest that there are cognitive therapies in where both chemical balance and the reintroduction of the management of emotions, as well as harvesting the development of the brain has shown to have yielded positive results.

It is fundamental for a working society to work with every member of the public, in all walks of life in order to seek out improvement. Seeking out the potential for positive change. If there are neurological indicators that physical damage is not present, coupled with the suggestion that a display of emotions can be seen, then there is a basis of neurological development is not only possible, but plausible. There are significant indicators within all aspects of the mental health spectrum that people from all walks of life and disposition, are able to benefit from focussed forms of therapy.

While it can be conceded that in cases of physical neurological damage that there is little that can be done to repair the certain kinds of personality disorders. However, it would be remis to dismiss certain criminals, such as Serial Killers as being of nothing more than a particular type of personality diagnosis, when there are indicators being revealed through the means of research, in where we are constantly discovering new information regarding how the mind can work. New research brings new information, therefore, until we can prove that a person is beyond redemption in terms of remorse and guilt, then we should not stop searching when there are possibilities and indications there to be uncovered.

The human mind is a wonderful and fascinating thing to behold. There is such fascination with just how people can be inventive, as well as overcoming adversity in the most remarkable of situations. Us as humans never seem to stop in terms of what we are capable to learn, not only about others, but about ourselves as well. With this in mind, there are no limits as to what we can learn about the darkest and the lightest aspects of our characters. An approach with an open mind as to possibility may just provide a surprise that can be developed for the benefit of all.

In my discussions with a psychologist, I have put forward the plausibility of Serial Killers having the potential to feel remorse. To which there was a back-and-forth discussion as to the merits of the potential theory. The conversation moved in the direction of Cognitive Science, in where the process of observation was detailed from a human and naturalistic approach. The studies of people and their behaviours being that if a particular behaviour, unless there was a physical neurological reason relating to damaged areas of the brain, then there was the potential for developing learned behaviour, but also the possibility of unlearning negative behaviour as well.

With cognitive science and an approach to psychopathy, unless there is existing damage to the frontal lobes of the brain which essentially controls the aspects of emotion and impulse, then there is nothing to suggest that the neurons which send the signals to this section of the brain would not have the ability in which to revitalise the emergence of these emotions and impulses at different times. Therefore, even in the case of Serial Killers, if these types of people are without the physical damage to the frontal lobe, then there is evidence from a humanistic and cognitive point of view, that the possibility of feeling and showing of emotions such as guilt and remorse, are entirely plausible.

Sondra London

Bearing true witness.

Throughout history, it has been the eyewitness accounts and documentation of such events which give us the means to look at things and form an understanding in retrospect. Granted that the perception of history has been written by the victors when referenced to conflict, being the view that has been taken in terms of times of old, especially when the means of recording history was not as simplified as it is today.

For example, the vast majority of the information regarding the British Colonial Wars in places such as Africa for example, have been documented at the hands of British Scholars. The Anglo Zulu war in the South Eastern area of Africa in 1879 has been documented almost in its entirety from the side of the British accounts. While it is true that Tribal Chieftains such as Cetshwayo have been recorded in history, there is not as much recorded information about his victories, such as the battle of Isandlwana, as there is regarding his defeats. An example of which would be the famous battle of Rorke's Drift, in where Cetshwayo's army was defeated by Lieutenants Chard and Bromwell of the British Royal Engineers. The battle was immortalised in the 1964 Movie *Zulu* featuring Stanley Baker and Michael Caine.

Times closer to our present day have become slightly less biased in terms of the historic documentation of events, owing to the fact that the scope of media in which to record history has developed drastically in all countries across the world. For example, people who watch historical television documentaries these days, are able to discover footage from all parties involved in wars such as World War Two and the American involvement in Vietnam, mainly due to the fact that footage from both of these conflicts have been filmed at times, giving us a more in-depth account as to exactly what happened during both of these wars. It could be taken that the view point in which these documentary style of programs have been delivered to us, as well as the fictional movies which have been inspired by these events, are still being portrayed with a sense of bias (The majority of films regarding these wars are generally from the point of view of the British or Americans respectively), however, there is a lot more which we are able to decipher for ourselves in terms of opinion, owing to the fact that alternate footage is more available to us now than there once was in retrospect.

The same could be said with regards to the world of true crime. Our only accounts of historical Serial Killers, such as "Jack the Ripper" and slightly more recent killers such as John Reginald Christie, were both documented at times in where all we had to rely on for detailed information was the newspaper reporting of the time, as well as a limited account of potential speculation, due to the fact that members of the victim's families, or people that knew the suspected murderer were not interviewed in the same manner in which they are today.

Due to media coverage and the human interest which has developed with regards to the topic of true crime, the mindset of a true crime perpetrator has become a common interest for many. Countless documentaries have been shown to interview the families of the victims, as well as the Law Enforcement agencies which have apprehended those responsible for the crimes. Where there was still somewhat of a gap was, however, those who crossed the threshold and sought to gain information directly from the horse's mouth so to speak. Those who dared to take the words of a Serial Killer directly, to then publish into books so that the rest of the world could see the world of crime from an untold perspective.

I am talking of people such as the acclaimed Author, Sondra London. An author who has dared to cross the threshold and make it possible to platform the kinds of books relating to Serial Killers that we have today.

Sondra London was born in Florida in 1947 and is today known as one of the leading writers in terms of bringing an in-depth knowledge of True Crime accounts to our doorsteps. In fact, one could not delve into the world of True Crime publications without recognising her name as a pantheon amongst the bestsellers of the genre.

Having begun her career as a technical writer working for lawyers, as well as writing manuals for computer programming, Sondra turned her attention to the world of True Crime after having been in contact with G.J Schaefer, a man who was convicted of Serial Murder in 1973. It is suspected that Schaefer was responsible for more than thirty murders during his killing spree, although he has not been convicted for all of his crimes.

Sondra London had dated Schaefer in her youth, and it was upon hearing that her former High School boyfriend had, other than becoming a police officer, had been arrested on murder charges, it prompted London to contact Schaefer once again, to begin collaboration for the book which would be titled **Killer Fiction**.

During this time, Schaefer corresponded with Sondra London by way of prison visits and hand written letters, in where Schaefer divulged the details of the crimes and factors surrounding some of the murders which he had committed. Schaefer had denied his guilt in relation to any of the murders that he had been convicted of, going as far as to threaten to sue any persons who published any details of his crimes which would lay doubt as to his overall innocence. Schaefer's details of his crimes in relation to his collaboration with Sondra London, have always been portrayed by Schaefer as nothing more than an account of fiction. However, Sondra London has stated that Schaefer was in fact every bit of a Serial Killer that he had been portrayed to be. A statement which resulted in threats being made against Sondra's life in a repeated fashion, as well as a law suit which Schaefer filed against her for naming him as a Serial Killer in the publication. The law suit was ultimately dismissed by the courts.

Not only was this book one of the very first books which was able to provide any forms of insight into the mind of a Serial Killer, it was the work of Sondra London which was able to bring to conclusion some of the "Cold Cases" of murder victims who were found in the Ocala National Forrest in Florida, North of Orlando. Cases which may have never been able to have been solved if it were not for the assistance and insight of Sondra London.

Following her work on **Killer Fiction** with Schaefer, Sondra has continued to actively work on the genre of True Crime non-fiction with a variety of different publications. A collaboration with Dianne Fitzpatrick, in where they published a book called **Good Little Soldiers: A Memoir of True Horror**. This book tells the tale of true horror and murder, as well as Military Mind Control being used as a means of experimentation with the use of mind-altering drugs on Fitzpatrick and her brother, when they were only six years old. A programme that the siblings were enlisted in by their father, a homicidal maniac who was involved in the experiments at the time.

Other publications include **True Vampires**, a book which gives a documentation of various murderous accounts in where Vampirism has taken place in accordance with a killer's specific crimes. This book includes an account of Nicolas Claux, who in addition to being included in the book, also worked with Sondra London as a means to provide the illustrations for the publication. The very same Nicolas Claux who I have written the account of his life in my own book **Lord of the Dead – The Bloody tales of the Vampire of Paris**.

The most striking of Sondra London's publications could arguably be **The Making of a Serial Killer**, a book that is now available as a second edition. This book has been set based on the life of Danny Rolling, who was known as the "Gainesville Ripper". It was Rolling's crime spree which the now famous *Scream* movie franchise created by Horror producer Wes Craven, was originally based upon. Initially, Rolling was convicted of the crime of murdering five students who attended university in Gainesville, Florida between 1989 and 1990, as well as the rape and murder of another three victims in Louisiana, LA in 1989. For his crimes of murder, Rollings would eventually be put to death by lethal injection in October of 2006, at Florida State Prison.

While it is the account of Danny Rolling that is going to be the comparison which will be most apt for the plausibility for the theory of this book. It is to be noted that I am looking to avoid the use of direct quotation from the books of Sondra London. The reason being that, for one, that my making a connection between Danny Rolling and the theme of this book is entirely of my own understanding and not the potential misquoting of facts. The other reason being that I would encourage readers to obtain the works of Sondra London for themselves in order to gain their own insight from the stories in her books. In my correspondence with Sondra London, I have found her to be one of the most insightful persons whom I have had the privilege to speak with regarding the subject.

Whilst a view at her appearances on programmes such as Larry King Live, as well as the multitude of documentaries that she has appeared on, such as the UK's BBC, will show that she is not only extremely informed in her research on the genre, but she has been a pioneer in terms of crossing the divide between the world we submerse ourselves in, and the world of the Serial Killer. Without the works of Sondra London and the steps in she has taken to bring the mindset of the Serial Killer from the world of taboo to the comfort of our homes, there would have been no such pathways in which to have learned what we know today. Therefore, we are given the opportunity to make up our own minds, simply by reading the works of such a pacesetter in the genre of True Crime.

Danny Rolling has been noted as being an extremely disturbed individual who, when committing his crimes, had goals of eclipsing the notorious Ted Bundy in terms of setting numbers of his intended victims. It could be said that Rolling had wished for the equal, and potentially exceeding, notoriety of Ted Bundy. Although his number of murders did not surpass Bundy's in that respect, there is certainly a more in-depth view into the mind of a Serial Killer when studying Rolling, than there ever was with Bundy. The reason for that being that there was never the collaboration from Bundy with a writer, such as the one which Rolling undertook with

Sondra London for the book *The Making of a Serial Killer*. Sondra London's book gives us a front row view into Rolling's mind, far greater than any news reports from the time could ever have possibly wished for. These were Rolling's own words, crafted and narrated in a way that the world had never seen before and arguably, has not seen since. The drawings in the book were all done by Rolling, accompanying the in-depth details of each individual crime.

There has been speculation as to the personal relationship that Sondra London had with Danny Rolling at the time in where the information was gathered for the book, not to mention that there are so many variables in the book, that it would be impossible even to remotely cover the majority of them in this passage. In that respect, we are not going to do so. As stated previously, for a full in depth look into the life of Danny Rolling, I would urge you to purchase a copy of ***The making of a Serial Killer – Second edition*** for yourselves.

What I understood from the book was that Rolling was a complex character, even to himself. There were parts of his character that were undeniably brutal, which steered him in his compulsion to commit murder, as well as portions of his psyche which were at odds with the crimes that he was committing. In his accounts, there were times in where he would refrain from carrying out a particular murder, as his sense of guilt battled and overcame, his desire to take another's life. There are words from Rolling about not only his internal battle within himself, in where he was at the point of committing murder, to when he would be reminded of something such as a memory, which led to being overcome by a sense of remorse for the actions he was about to carry out. Remorse which led him to letting his

potential victim not only live but go free
from his grasp entirely.

Rolling spoke of love, his faith, as well as
how he understood his personality to be split
into what I understood to be three separate
entities of himself. He understood that he
had a destructive side, as well as a side of
him which was capable of remorse, as well as
showing aspects of creativity, which is
displayed in not only his drawings, but also
in the fact that, at the point of his impending
execution, he was able to recite a Christian
Hymn which he had written himself. This
Hymn sent out a gospel message of love.

Rolling was given, as with so many other
Serial Killers, the diagnosis of being an
Antisocial Personality Disorder. A diagnosis
which lends itself to the plausibility that the
person suffering from such a diagnosis would
be unable to understand, feel, or even display

emotions such as guilt or remorse. However, from my understanding of his own words, this is not entirely accurate. It has been stated on several occasions that Rolling was indeed conflicted by the very emotions that he is said to have not been able to feel.

There is nothing in this to suggest that these feelings that Rolling was said to have been conflicted by, were not disorientated in his overall psychological understanding of himself. However, that does not mean that these feelings of guilt and remorse were not present. Therefore, it does cast doubt as to whether or not the diagnosis of being an Antisocial Personality Disorder has once again been placed as the blanket, or generalised diagnosis of a Serial Killer when there are clear indications that further and individual examination could have been done for Danny Rolling.

This is in no way a means to suggest that the penalty of death for his crimes was not warranted, as the punishment of the death penalty is one for an individual's own set of values to decide upon as being for, or against such a punishment. This is merely to state that although the crimes were heinous in nature, making the blanket statement that the individual was not able to feel or display remorse or guilt is something that has been perhaps overlooked.

My conclusion when looking into the life and crimes of Danny Rolling, is that the crimes that he committed were just as they were reported, in that they were horrific in nature. However, it is easy to overlook the other aspects of his life and psychological state as the murders that he committed cast a vast shadow over the other aspects of his persona. A shadow that, as is the case with a great number of Serial Killers, has a tendency to dismiss the human side of the killer in question. It is understandable that the sensationalism of certain crimes makes it easier to discard these Serial Killers as monsters, as it creates a distinction in the minds of law-abiding citizens that they are in no way similar to the "monsters" which are read about in reports and seen on the television. While this may be true in terms of behaviours of an individual, it is plausible that dismissing the fact that some of these Serial Killers are able to understand and display a wide set of emotions is an incorrect way of looking at these types of people within our societies.

The works of Sondra London in these cases, has for me, and I am sure a great deal many others, given an alternate perspective in the way that we are able to view Serial Killers. While it may not be the intention of the writer to create such a question. The same can be said for people such as musicians.

A musician will often write a song with their own emotions and viewpoints in mind, but that does not mean that the listener will take the same message from the song in the way that the musician intended. In that respect, the work of Sondra London can be likened to the musical equivalent of True Crime writing. In where the talent and composition of the writing has been done in a manner in which to draw in the reader to the intelligence and dedication to the art. To then be in the valued position of leaving us to create our own understandings.

The works of people such as Sondra London are invaluable in the fact that we are provided with the opportunity in which to be able to gain an alternate view into the mind of a Serial Killer. As without her works, there would be so much that would remain unknown to the reader. It may not have been highlighting a potential for guilt or remorse that was her intention when writing the books, however, I am grateful that there is the opportunity to be able to grasp such a concept through an alternate perspective. Like all people who follow their favourite musician, there is much to be gained from following the works of Sondra London, as you can never anticipate just what it is that you will come to understand in the next book.

It is with that understanding, that Sondra London's work is a key fundamental factor in the world of true crime literature, as the genre would not be the same without her books.

Gary Ridgeway – The Green River Killer

A bold move by the Authorities?

The subject of clemency or leniency is one that is often met with a great deal of scrutiny. Especially in cases where the majority of the public feel that the application of leniency to an offender has been issued, without taking the magnitude of the crimes into account. The example in this instance being the crime of murder.

On occasion, in the countries which have the Death Penalty as the mandatory punishment for the crime of murder, a ruling Judge, or even the prosecuting body themselves, will remove the penalty of death as the ultimate form of punishment, if there are extenuating circumstances in the case. For example, an offender may offer up a guilty plea to their crimes, if there is a guarantee that the prosecution will not seek out the death penalty during the trial. In these cases, the offender often knows that the case that the prosecution has against them is one that will determine their guilt beyond all reasonable doubt. In cases such as these, the offender understands that there is an overwhelming possibility that they are going to be found guilty, regardless of whatever defence strategy that their lawyers may wish to proceed with. Therefore, the better option for the offender is to make a deal with the prosecution so that their punishment is reduced as much as possible. It is a case of damage limitation, as best they can.

In other instances, as is often the case with serial murderers, there are possibilities that the offender may have committed more murders than they are ultimately being charged with, (Ted Bundy was initially convicted of three murders in Florida, however, he had been connected to at least thirty in total), as a result, the prosecution team often offer up a lenient sentence in the hope that the murderer will assist the authorities in solving the remaining "cold cases".

Controversy is never out of reach when a sentence of leniency is handed out by the courts, for a number of reasons. The families of the victims often feel that the person responsible for the murders had showed no mercy for the victims, therefore, the murderer should in turn, be shown the same lack of mercy when it comes to the punishment that they ultimately receive for the crimes. As a result, there is often an outcry of disapproval from the families of the victims when leniency is shown, as they feel that justice for their loved ones has not been delivered. In addition, the public are often equally outraged in cases such as these, as the public wish to feel safe and secure in understanding that the authorities are doing enough to ensure the safety of the local citizens is being done.

When a Serial Killer's case is in the news, there is often a large degree of highly charged emotions present, from the families of the victims, as well as the public who either directly or indirectly, have a vested interest in the understanding that they are being represented correctly by the justice system which they trust to look after their safety and security. Therefore, the emotional levels that people may feel when there is a court case for a person suspected of serial murder is always going to be heightened beyond the average when compared to crimes of another nature.

Should there be an ongoing case into serial murder which exceeds what is considered to be prolific, then the levels of heightened emotion will in turn, be excessive in nature as well. Therefore, when a Serial Killer such as Gary Ridgeway, also known as the "Green River Killer", a man who is arguably one of the most prolific Serial Killers in American history hits the news, then all precedents are null and void in terms of emotion. As we are now entering unchartered territory with someone such as Gary Ridgeway.

Gary Ridgeway was born on the 18th of February 1949 in Salt Lake City, Utah. Ultimately, Ridgeway would go on to become one of, if not the most prolific Serial Killers in modern history. His killing spree would start in 1982 and go on for almost two decades in total. A killing spree that, although Ridgeway having been initially convicted of murdering forty-eight people, has been estimated to be as high as seventy-one, according to confessions made by Ridgeway following his imprisonment.

The Ridgeway family moved from Salt Lake City to Seattle, Washington when Gary was very young. Despite being born in a location where the ideals of church life were prevalent, it has been documented that Gary Ridgway had led a troubled childhood, with a vast majority of the issues that he faced in life stemming from a dysfunctional family environment.

In the family home, Ridgeway was witness to frequent arguments between his parents, arguments which often resulted in violent behaviour. Although, authorities were never reported to having been called to stem the violence which the young Gary Ridgeway was subjected to witnessing. The negativity that surrounded Ridgeway did not stop at merely witnessing his parents argue. His father was a bus driver and as a result, had to drive through the more deprived areas of Seattle, in where his father would witness the influx of sex workers such as prostitutes, in the area. His father disapproved of the presence of these sex workers, however, rather than keeping his displeasure quiet when he returned home, he was often vocal in his negative views on the subject. These negative and descriptive views were not shielded from the young boy's ears. Instead, Gary Ridgeway was subjected to detailed information on what it was that these sex workers were doing, despite his age being one that would not have been able to process the information in the same manner as that of an adult.

In addition, Ridgeway was known to having been a bed wetter. This unfortunate trait started in his infancy and continued into his teenage years. Upon each occasion that Ridgeway would wet the bed, his mother would wash his genitals, even in his adolescent years. This is a trait which would not have been uncommon for any young child who was unfortunate to have wet the bed, however, as a teenager, it would be considered to be degrading and humiliating.

It is unclear as to whether or not the words of his father with regards to the views on sex workers would have had an emotional effect in his early teenage years, however, Ridgeway has confessed that his mother's actions with regards to the washing of his genitals after each bed wetting incident, did in fact leave him with an inner sense of conflict. As Ridgeway has admitted to feeling the contradiction of emotions towards his mother, in terms of a confusion between identifying having had sexual attraction towards his mother, as well as anger and fantasies of wanting to kill her as a result of the degradation he felt when he was forced to having his genitals washed. Especially in the manner that his mother had done it.

Considering that the vast majority of Gary Ridgeway's victims were comprised of sex workers and prostitutes, as well as women who could have been deemed to be from vulnerable backgrounds, there is suggestion that the aspects of both of his parent's behaviour could have played a fundamental part in Ridgeway's ultimate devolution to murder.

At the age of twenty, Ridgeway was married to his High School girlfriend and had enlisted in the United States Navy. Even though he had, at the age of sixteen, lured a six-year-old boy into the local woods and stabbed him through the lungs, penetrating the child's liver. Despite this event in his teenage years, Ridgeway was accepted into the Navy and subsequently, sent to Vietnam, as the War between the United States and Vietnam was still ongoing.

While in Vietnam, Ridgeway was subjected to witnessing conflict and violence, despite having been deployed to serve on a Navy supply ship. While ashore, Ridgeway would frequently engage in the services of local prostitutes. From these encounters, Ridgeway contracted a sexually transmitted disease, something which angered him. However, despite holding feelings of anger towards prostitutes, he continued to engage in sexual encounters with them, without taking the measures to use protection, or even have the sexually transmitted disease treated medically.

Upon returning home, the actions which Ridgeway had indulged in while in Vietnam caused his marriage to his young wife to dissolve. The couple soon divorced. Ridgeway has been married a total of three times (from which he has one child to his second wife) and every one of his wives have made similar statements regarding Gary Ridgeway's behaviour, in that he was said to have an insatiable sexual appetite, often demanding sex several times a day, as well as his second wife making the claim that Ridgeway had displayed violence towards her, by way of trying to choke or strangle her. Further to this, each of his wives have stated that a major problem within the relationships was that Ridgeway was often guilty of infidelity. Although, the infidelity within his first two marriages were not entirely one sided, as there had been infidelity on the part of his first two wives as well. A notion which added to the devolving anger that Ridgeway had developed towards women.

Considering that Gary Ridgeway's second wife has claimed that he had attempted to strangle her by means of a chokehold, it is not surprising that strangulation, either by hand or by ligature, was the primary method in which he had chosen to murder his victims.

During his second marriage, Ridgeway had become involved in the church. He began reciting passages from the bible while both at work and in the home. He even went as far as to travel from door to door, preaching the word of God in his local neighbourhood. It has been said that Ridgeway would become emotional after reading sermons from the bible, going as far as to even weep upon the completion of a bible passage. Despite his love for the church and the word of God, Ridgeway had not refrained from the services of sex workers and prostitutes. Giving rise to the suggestion that he had developed an inner conflict between his insatiable lust for women and his religious beliefs.

Ridgeway had started his killing spree in 1982, killing up to seventy-one teenage girls near both Tacoma and Seattle in the Washington area. His first five victims were dumped and then discovered in Seattle's Green River, hence the media dubbed moniker of the "Green River Killer". His victims comprised mainly of teenage girls who were working in the sex industry as prostitutes. Ridgeway would lure the girls back to either his home, his truck, or on occasion, a secluded area, in where he would murder the girls by strangulation. The lure that he used on the girls was to avail of their services for sex, however, unbeknownst to the girls, his ultimate motive would be murder.

Ridgeway would first engage in sex with the girls, before strangling them to death. He has stated that during sex, he would wrap his arm around the neck of the girl while he was placed behind them, while pushing their back's forward with the other arm. Choking them out until he was sure that they had stopped breathing. A manoeuvre which would ultimately become his signature in terms of identifying these victims as having been murdered by the same perpetrator.

Following having dumped his initial victims in or around the banks of the Green River, this would no longer be a suitable disposal site for his victims as the press and authorities had become aware of the river as the disposal site. Therefore, Ridgeway was forced to find other areas in which to rid himself of the deceased girls. Ridgeway opted for secluded areas in the King County within Washington state, as these were areas that he could dispose of the bodies with a degree of personal safety, but also so that he would be able to return to these dumpsites so that he could repeatedly have sex with the decomposing corpses of the young prostitutes.

Ridgeway has stated that there was no overwhelming desire to have sex with the corpses of the deceased girls, as it was no more satisfying for him to indulge in necrophilia than it was to have sex with a living person. However, as he had the means to continue his sexual exploits with the corpses, it meant that he was able to indulge and satisfy his sexual urges without the requirement to kill more victims. Often, Ridgeway would not kill another victim until the corpse of his latest victim was decomposed to the point in where it was no longer suitable to satisfy his sexual appetite.

There had been large amounts of crime scene contamination left at the disposal sites of Ridgeway's victims. However, at this point in time, there was not the technology available as there is today in where Ridgeway could have been connected to the murders. In the early stages of the Police investigation, Ridgeway was identified as a person of interest, however, there was not sufficient evidence to connect him to the crimes, therefore, this was not an avenue in which the Police initially followed up on.

One of the most remarkable aspects of this investigation is that the task force, led by Robert D Keppel, who was a part of the King's Country Sheriff's department at the time, worked with Ted Bundy in a means to create a profile as to identify the Green River Killer. As we already know, Robert D Keppel is one of the highest acclaimed profilers and criminal investigators that both King County and the F.B.I has ever had on their books. Keppel had recognised that they were in need of assistance with regards to discovering the identity of the Green River Killer and as such, understood that a killer of Ted Bundy's ilk, would be best positioned as to shine a light on the mindset of such a killer. Although Ridgeway was not apprehended prior to Bundy's execution in 1989, Bundy's assistance was pivotal in creating a suitable and working profile for the Green River case.

With one of the most valuable pieces of information that Bundy provided was that there was a strong possibility that the Green

River Killer would possibly return to the dumpsites and therefore, the dumpsites that the police discovered, should be monitored for the killer's return.

Ridgeway had been arrested in 1982 on prostitution related charges and as a result, he was suspected as having involvement in the Green River Killings in 1983 (Ridgeway had passed a polygraph test in 1984). In 1987, with the murder cases still no closer to being resolved, the police decided to re-trace their retrospective leads by taking saliva and hair samples from persons of interest. As having been on the police radar for these crimes, the police opted to take samples from Gary Ridgeway.

In 2001, the police had begun to profile the samples of hair and saliva that they had taken from persons of interest with regard to the Green River Killings, testing all of the samples that they had collected against DNA evidence which they had collected from four of the bodies of the victims which had been discovered. As a result, Ridgeway's samples provided a match against the collected DNA. On the 30th of November 2001, Police arrived at his place of work and arrested Ridgeway for the murders of the four young girls.

In November 2003, Ridgeway entered a plea of guilty to forty-eight counts of first-degree murder following confessing to the prosecution for the Green River Killings. His confession to the crimes was done as part of a plea which would spare Gary Ridgeway the punishment of the death penalty. In exchange for his confessions, Ridgeway agreed to a sentence of leniency. The sentence being that instead of the death penalty, Ridgeway would serve forty-eight life sentences, without ever having the possibility for parole.

In a statement made by the prosecution team, the authorities having tested Ridgeway's DNA against all of the other cold case files that they were working on, they could only potentially link Gary Ridgeway to seven of the discovered victims. Therefore, in a means to bring closure to the families of the remaining forty-one victims that they had on file, the plea deal of commuting Ridgeway's sentence from that of the death penalty to life imprisonment, was not a decision that was made for the benefit of Ridgeway. It had been noted that certain factions of the prosecution have stated that Ridgeway did not deserve the courts mercy or leniency, however, as they were putting the thoughts of the victim's families first, the leniency was done so that Ridgeway's confession would bring peace to the mourning families.

During the sentencing portion of Gary Ridgeway's trial, the judge had allowed the families of the victims to make statements with regards to their feelings, towards Ridgeway. Almost all of the family members of the victims stated their distain, disgust, and anger towards the now identified Green River Killer. All but one made disparaging remarks about what they thought of Ridgeway. The one who chose not to make negative remarks, chose to forgive Ridgeway for his crimes, as this was the Christian thing to do. Following these remarks, as well as Ridgeways own statement in where he stated that he was sorry and remorseful of not only his crimes, but also the effect that his crimes had brought the victims' families. The Judge stated that he did not believe the remorse shown by Ridgeway, making the statement that he found Ridgeway to be nothing more than a cold, remorseless killer.

It is these statements by the victims' families in where the case for Gary Ridgeway and the potential for genuine remorse can be identified. It has been said in Psychological studies that a person who feels genuine hatred for themselves, will welcome any forms of a barrage of verbal abuse towards themselves, as in a manner of speaking, they believe that the abuse that they are subjected to, was warranted and in turn, actually makes themselves feel better for being spoken to in the manner which they feel that they deserve. It is only when the family member of the victim who chose to forgive him, do we see the wall of self-loathing begin to crumble from Ridgeway. The man's words of forgiveness seemed to penetrate the emotional wall that Ridgeway had built, which caused not only genuine tears from Ridgeway, but the trembling of Ridgeway's lower lip, which can be seen as physical attribute to an emotion of genuine remorse.

Ridgeway has stated that during his nearly two decades of a killing spree, there were gaps in where his murderous antics went dormant. Usually this happens when a serial killer has been apprehended for another crime and as such, is unable to continue their crimes due to being incarcerated for another, unrelated crime. Psychologists have stated that a killer of Ridgeway's ilk, would be unable to refrain from murder, as they don't have the mental capacity in which to just "stop" killing. This is not the case with Gary Ridgeway. Over his nigh on twenty year killing spree, there were portions of time, as much as up to four years, in where Ridgeway did not commit any murders, nor was he incarcerated. In his own words Ridgeway has stated that the reason for the halt in killing, was because he was happy within his family life.

For a person who is apparently unable to process emotions such as love, guilt, remorse etc, this is not meant to be possible. The fact is that Ridgeway has been said to having displayed all of these emotions. Further studies into the words of Ridgeway give indication that he in fact *is* able to display remorse and understand the gravity of his crimes. In the latter parts of his killing spree, Ridgeway has stated that he started to bury the corpses of his victims as a means to deter him from returning to the dump sites in order to perform necrophilia on the dumped bodies. This has the hallmarks of a person who understands that the killings that he has committed, were not done as the result of a lack of remorse, but instead out of compulsion. The reason that he was able to silence his compulsions was that Ridgeway was in control of his emotions at a time in his life when he was in fact *happy*. The fact that he only resumed his murderous antics was when his marriages began to deteriorate, meant that the feelings of happiness dissipated, leaving Ridgeway open to submitting to his compulsions.

Owing to the fact that Gary Ridgeway was conflicted between the sexual attraction and rage that he felt towards his mother as a result of the degradation he suffered as a child, coupled with the mixture of processing the sentiments towards prostitutes inherited from his father, as well as the seemingly love-hate relationship that Ridgeway himself had developed as a result of his time spent with prostitutes while serving in Vietnam, means that this inner conflict was compartmentalised towards the sex workers that he ultimately murdered. The difference being that while this compartmentalisation was taking place, Ridgeway was unable to control his emotions as a result of his inner conflict. However, that does not mean that there is an absence of human emotion, but rather that Ridgeway was unable to control the emotions that he felt at the time.

The presence of human emotion by Ridgeway does not mean that he should be exonerated for his crimes of murder. Instead, with the lack of control of these emotions it provides enough insight that Ridgeway would continue to serve as a danger to others if he were not in prison. Therefore, the fact that he has no option other than to spend the remainder of his life incarcerated, it is the correct one. Looking at his youth and key moments in his life it is evident just as to where the pivotal moments in his ultimate devolution towards murder began, however, there is still so much that could be learned from the mind of Gary Ridgeway. His inner conflict alone gives enough evidence that his case could be used into research into the prevention of similar Serial Killers in the future.

Therefore, the option for leniency or mercy in the case of Gary Ridgeway, further than providing closure to the families of the victims, could be proved to have been the correct decision. As it is clear that there is still so much that we have the ability to learn.

From my own correspondence with letters written both to and return by Ridgeway, he has openly admitted that his mindset is one as far from murder and crime and in turn, has devoted his life and heart to God once again. He has accepted his fate and tries to promote the workings of the church.

David Berkowitz – The Son of Sam

The Dawn that follows the Darkness.

The saying of "The light at the end of the tunnel is that of an oncoming train" is one that we hear frequently in our day to day lives. The general premise for this saying is that when we sometimes think that we are nearing a potential positive outlet during dark times, but there is an equal but opposite potential that the light may not be the salvation which we had hoped for, instead that the road ahead could be fraught with disaster and dangers.

Being the eternal optimist, as well as always looking for potential alternate views, there is always a different way of looking at things, even with age-old sayings such as the one that has just been given as an example.

A simple side step of the potential oncoming disaster and the train approaching becomes a threat to your safety no more. In fact, should you find a means to board the train, then the possibility of going on a voyage of discovery becomes a viable alternative. Granted that the destination of the train or the voyage would be somewhat unknown, however, as there is the guiding light of the train highlighting all that lays ahead on your path, there is an opportunity to look ahead and see the path ahead before you reach that point in your journey.

Should the path ahead not be one that you deem to be favourable, then there is nothing to stop you from stepping down from the train, to attempt to try and alternative route. It could be understood that prior to this, the train may have caused some destruction to those who were caught up in the train's momentum, however, that does not mean that there would be similar destruction that lays ahead. Yes, there may have been a destructive path which the train that followed, however, thanks to the shining light of the train, there is a chance to avoid negativity and opt to try and discover the potential for an alternate and bright future instead.

It is understandable to find it difficult to apply this metaphor to that of a Serial Killer. However, that does not mean that there is not an example of such a bright light to be had. In fact, with the result of research, correspondence with a convicted killer, as well as correspondence with a killer's representatives, the opportunity to discover that bright light in the world of the Serial Killer has been made possible.

David Richard Berkowitz was born in June of 1953 in Brooklyn, New York. Berkowitz was born illegitimately to a Jewish-American mother, who gave him up for adoption after his birth. Berkowitz was then adopted by another Jewish-American family who were based in the Bronx area of New York City. His birth mother was said to having been involved in a relationship with a married man at the time, therefore, was not in a position to name who the father of her child was.

Berkowitz has been documented as being something of a troubled child. As he was the only child of his adoptive parents, it has been said that he was often spoiled and was given his own way on most occasions. This led to Berkowitz being noted as developing into something of a difficult child, often becoming a bully to others around him. Despite his behaviour not having been significantly documented on school records, it has been noted that his adoptive parents had sought out the help of a psychologist, in an attempt at curtailing Berkowitz's disruptive behaviour.

Berkowitz was said to have had flirtations with theft and robberies, as well as the reckless behaviour of starting fires. His home life became troubled when, at the age of fourteen, his adoptive mother died of breast cancer. The relationship between Berkowitz and his adoptive father became strained as a result, even further so as it was said that Berkowitz did not like his adoptive father's second wife. Although he had lived with his adoptive father following his adoptive mother's death, Berkowitz left to join the United States Army in 1971.

Berkowitz served at the post of Fort Knox in the United States and in South Korea, as a member of the infantry. In 1974 he was honourably discharged from the army, to which he then decided to locate his biological mother. Upon being reunited with his mother, he was informed of the details of his birth. The apparent lack of a consistent father figure seemed to have caused Berkowitz a great deal of emotional pain, which with the full account of the details of his birth and lack of a paternal figure, was a catalyst in becoming the first known "crisis" or "stressor" in his life.

His reunification with his mother began to lapse following this information that he had received, although Berkowitz has remained in contact with his half-sister. Berkowitz then enrolled himself in college, as well as having a series of low profile, menial jobs, such as working for the postal service, as well as working a New York Taxi driver.

From 1975, Berkowitz began to commit violent crimes. His first crime was to stab two young women in Co-op city in New

York. He stabbed the two victims with a hunting knife on Christmas eve. One of the victims never came forward to the authorities about the attack, however, the other, a fifteen-year-old student called Michelle Forman, sustained serious injuries from the knife attack. She was subsequently hospitalised for seven days, though she was not able to identify her attacker at the time.

Berkowitz had discovered that the attempt to murder another person by use of the hunting knife was too difficult an ordeal for him, therefore, he devolved from the use of the knife to that of a .44 Calibre hand gun. Regardless of the choice of weapon that Berkowitz chose to use for his attacks, what was the most notable fact of his crimes were, that he chose to attack two victims simultaneously on each occasion. Further to this, it had been noted that Berkowitz often returned to the scenes of his crimes, as it has been said that he took pleasure in the reminiscing of the attacks, by way of revisiting the scenes.

The first of his attacks by use of the .44 Calibre handgun, was on the 29th of July 1976. Berkowitz visited the Pelham Bay area of the Bronx. Berkowitz approached a car that was parked at the side of the road, the two occupants were sitting inside of the car, discussing the events of their evening to that point. Berkowitz surprised the occupants of the car by approaching them, then pulling his handgun out from a concealed paper bag. He shot one of the occupants in the head, killing them instantly. The second person, he shot in the thigh, wounding them. Upon having finished his attack, Berkowitz turned away and walked briskly away from the scene.

Although the occupant of the car was able to survive their attack, they were not able to identify their attacker. They were able to give police a brief description of Berkowitz, stating that he was about 1.7 metres tall and weighed an approximate 200lbs. He was described as being a white male with a fair complexion, as well as having a dark but short, curly hairstyle. The surviving victim's father, who was near the shooting at the time, described Berkowitz as having a similar description, as well as driving a small yellow car. A notable piece of information, as neighbours of the victim had described a similar, but unfamiliar looking car patrolling the streets of the neighbourhood, some hours earlier.

The next shooting was on the 23rd of October 1976 in the area of Flushing, Queens, New York. Two people were once again sitting in a parked car at the side of the road, when Berkowitz began shooting at the parked car. One of the occupants were hit in the head by one of the shots, while the other occupant of the car suffered only superficial injuries as a result of the broken glass, shattered by the forage of bullets. Despite being hit in the head by the bullet, the occupant was able to escape to safety from the onslaught of Berkowitz. The victim survived the attack, however, they needed to have a metal plate surgically installed as a means to repair the damage of the bullet. Neither of the occupants of the car were able to catch a glimpse of Berkowitz and therefore, were unable to provide an accurate description. What was unusual in this instance, was that in this attack, the driver of the car was male. All of Berkowitz's attacks up until this point were aimed at female victims. The male victim did, however, have long hair, which may have Berkowitz the impression that the occupant of the car was a female. The other aspect of this shooting was that it was not initially connected to Berkowitz's previous attacks, as they were in different boroughs of the city, therefore there was no connection as to the attacks having been carried out by the same perpetrator.

The majority of Berkowitz's victims seemed to follow the same modus operandi, in that the majority of his victims were female in his initial attacks, as well as being sat in parked cars at the times of the attacks. There were of course exceptions to this pattern, as the killing spree went on, several males were targeted, however, this was mainly due to the fact that certain media outlets had labelled Berkowitz as a "woman-hater". While it could have been the press releases in connection to the killings that changed his victimology, it seems as though opportunity also played a role in changing his M.O from people being attacked while sitting in parked cars.

As in March of 1977, Berkowitz shot and killed a female student who was walking

home from school in the evening. Berkowitz
shot at the young girl, who in an attempt to
defend herself from the forthcoming attack,
held her books up to protect her face. The
books did little to prevent harm, as the bullet
penetrated the books, passing through and
hitting her in the head, killing her instantly.

Initially the press had dubbed Berkowitz as
the ".44Calibre Killer", his name being given
to him in accordance with the type of
handgun that he had been using to carry out
the killings. It was suspected, although not
substantiated, that the same .44 Calibre
Bulldog Handgun had been used in all of the
attacks. The New York Post and Daily News
tabloids had given the case extensive
coverage on nearly a daily basis.

It was only after a letter addressed to the
Police was left at one of the murder scenes,
in where Berkowitz had named himself as

the "Son of Sam" as opposed to the woman-hating figure, or the ".44 Calibre Killer" which he had been referred to as previously. The letter to the police was written in something akin to broken English and initially the Police had suspected the language used in the letter to be an equivalent of a Scottish-English written dialect. The letter spoke of a seeming blood lust in terms of murder, however, the letter seemed to also contradict itself in terms of a strange attitude towards not only the police, but also of a love for the people of the Queens region of New York.

While it is a common trait amongst Serial Killers in that there is a desire to not only communicate with the public and media, but there is also an undercurrent of a desire in which to control the media as a source of power. The letter was strange in nature, as quotes from the letter stating that the Son of Sam was compelled to "Honour thy Father", his father being "Sam" by way of carrying out these attacks, despite going against his own love for the lives of the locals he was killing. In the letter, Berkowitz pleaded for the authorities to stop him, as he knew that he would kill again. Experts who studied the letter came to the conclusion that not only did the Son of Sam suffer from a potential form of "demonic possession", but also there was a possibility that he was a paranoid Schizophrenic.

A Son of Sam task force was set up to discover the identity of and capture, the unknown Berkowitz. The killings continued, as did the letters to the media. In May of 1977, an American journalist and author, Jimmy Breslin, was sent a letter from the Son of Sam, which he then handed over to the Police in New York. In this letter, Berkowitz spoke of social decay within New York, as well as making claims as to "Sam's handiwork", which is a direct description of the murders that he had committed. The letter spoke of reference to the 1973 Hammer Horror movie "The Wicker Man" as well as aspects of the letter almost being identified as biblical in nature, giving reference to the urban decay he witnessed on the streets of New York. The most disturbing aspect of the letter was the suggestion that on the 29th of July, there was going to be another murder committed by him. Up until that point, the majority of the victims of Berkowitz had long dark hair, therefore giving a suggestion that this was a benchmark in his victimology. The release of this detail, coupled with the fact that a prophecy of another killing being imminent, led to city wide panic among woman of that disposition. Creating a "panic sale" rush for items such as wigs as to disguise their own long and dark hair, as to eliminate themselves as a potential victim.

The killings continued in New York. It was only when a person had noticed a traffic warden placing a ticket on the window of a 1970 Ford Galaxie that was parked next a fire hydrant on the 31st of July 1977, in the area where the person later heard the gunshots of what would turn out to be Berkowitz's final victims, that any suspicion as to his identity was raised. Out of a sense of fear, the person who had heard the shots being fired, waited a total of four days before reporting it to the local police. The police having gathered the information from the bystander, searched through their records as to what yellow cars had been given a parking ticket on that night. David Berkowitz's name appeared in their research. The following day the Police decided to investigate Berkowitz and his car, in where they discovered a bag containing ammunition as well as maps of the crime scenes. The Police then obtained a search warrant so that their findings would not be able to be challenged in court. On the 10th of August 1977, David Berkowitz was arrested, having been found with a bag of ammunition next to him in his car. The .44 Calibre ammunition which matched the ammunition used in the Son of Sam Killings.

When Berkowitz was arrested, the police officer asked him who he was, to which Berkowitz replied, "You know". The conversation continued, with Berkowitz making the statements "I am Sam" and "Sam. David Berkowitz".

Berkowitz quickly confessed to being the Son of Sam killer. In where he quickly made the statement that his neighbours' dog (his neighbour was called Sam Carr, potentially where the Son of "Sam" came from?), a black Labrador that was possessed by a Demon, with the Demon subsequently giving Berkowitz the instruction to go out and kill. There were continued claims of demonic possession made by Berkowitz, as well as continued access to direct media coverage in which to give his story to the tabloids.

Finally, Berkowitz made the admission that he was not possessed, nor instructed to kill by a dog, clarifying that his claims were nothing more than a hoax. He went on to make the statement that he felt compelled to kill for a long period of time, as he had felt let down by a world which seems to have rejected him.

Despite statements made regarding Berkowitz's mental health, he was adjudged to be competent in which to stand trial. However, as the trial was beginning, Berkowitz tried to jump from the window of the court buildings, making claims that his last victim was "nothing but a whore" and that he would love to "kill her again", that he would love to "kill them all again".

Berkowitz was subsequently sentenced to serve a twenty-five years to life term for each of the six murdered victims, as well as the ten additional people that he had attempted murder. Initially, he was sent to a psychiatric prison unit, although it has been said that he struggled to cope with his new surroundings. He was transferred to various different prisons on a number of occasions, but ultimately has been sent to Shawangunk Correctional Facility in Ulster County, New York. Where he had been imprisoned ever since. Prior to his relocation to Shawangunk, Berkowitz has made claims as being a member of a Satanic Cult, as well as having co-conspirators in relation to the killings, although he has since refuted these allegations. Following a knife attack inside of prison on Berkowitz by another inmate, which not only nearly claimed his life, but also had the requirement for Berkowitz to receive more than fifty surgical stitches. He has since turned his life around, making the claim that he had received the attack inside of the prison that he had deserved. This near-death experience, giving Berkowitz the understanding of the error of his ways and as such, he has devoted his life since 1987, to Christianity. He has since divorced himself from the moniker of the "Son of Sam" and instead chooses to go by the name of the "Son of Hope", which is now more fitting to his Christian Beliefs.

The turnaround in the attitude in Berkowitz is like none other that we have witnessed when it comes to the world of the Serial Killer. Since 1987 Berkowitz has devoted his life to not only the church and Jesus Christ, but also to helping as many people as he can with regards to turning their lives around, away from the lifestyle of a world of crime. It is remarkable that a person who had once caused the entire city of New York to be on alert due to his killing spree, to having spent the last thirty-four years of his life devoted to bringing positivity to others.

Berkowitz had been diagnosed as being a paranoid Schizophrenic. Even in recent documentaries there has been professors and psychiatrists that stand by this diagnosis. Yet, in the study of Schizophrenia, it has been stated that this is a condition, while manageable, cannot be conventionally cured. In interviews with Berkowitz for television documentaries, Berkowitz himself has stated that he does not believe this to be the case, as it has been his understanding that psychiatrists have had a tendency to look at the person whom they are diagnosing and take their findings to fit a particular mould, as opposed to accurately diagnosing the patient in front of them. Berkowitz's theory on this matter seems accurate, as not only does he not display these psychological attributes these days, but in fact he views his actions at the time of his arrest as being as though it was done in another life. As he is as far removed from these actions today as is humanly possible. Considering that paranoid Schizophrenia is not something that can be reversed, there is little to suggest that his schizophrenia just "went away". It is far more plausible that the diagnosis was inaccurate to begin with, especially as there is suggestion that it was more convenient to fit the traits or symptoms that Berkowitz displayed, into a "box" to suit a narrative.

Berkowitz has displayed an immense amount of remorse for his crimes. He understands that he feels that he deserves to spend his life behind bars, as it is the correct punishment for the crimes that he has committed. His explanations of the polar opposite mindsets that he held from the time of his killing spree to that of his current views on life are completely different. He views himself in modern times to feeling as though he has a new life, with his former life of killing being completely foreign to him.

His work that he has been doing for people whilst in prison is being done in a manner in where he is able to *physically* show that he is sorry for his actions, as opposed to merely uttering the words. Despite the work that Berkowitz has been doing, he refuses to take credit for the lives that he has helped, stating that it is not himself that is responsible for the positivity, but instead it is God who deserves the praise. In his view, he is merely doing God's work, in order to better the lives of others.

Berkowitz talks openly about family life, especially with regards to the people that he has encountered and helped while inside of prison. He has taken up a role of a church minister, using this as the platform in which to help fellow inmates inside of the prison. He has implemented the mindset of inmates not to view their prison sentences as being a punishment, but rather an opportunity to rehabilitate not only their actions, but their lives. Using the prison sentence as a time for reflection as a means to better their lives upon ultimately being released from prison.

With the exception of the book **Murder in Mind**, where Berkowitz has admitted to telling the person who was writing the book what they wanted to hear, as opposed to what was really going on his mind at the time. Berkowitz has worked tirelessly on spreading his positivity and the word of God in publications across the world. His message to the world since 1987 has been one of hope, which is why he adopted the moniker of the "Son of Hope" to be in direct contrast to his previous Son of Sam identity. In addition, his website, www.ariseandshine.org which is run by his representatives, tells of a message of enduring positivity, as well as a heartfelt apology to all that had been affected by his actions. The website even going as far to state Berkowitz's words of, despite still being incarcerated, "I was once a prisoner, but now I'm free!" This reference does not mean that he has been let out of prison, but instead it is a statement that explains that he is free from the grasp of evil. Despite being walled up inside of a prison cell, he feels as though his soul is free and full of love. In addition to this, there are countless testimonies from Berkowitz on his positive outlook, as well as making the claim that he will continue to devote his life to spreading the word of God.

It is a common trait for people who have been incarcerated to find God inside of prison walls. It is often dismissed as nothing more than a gimmick in where people believe that the sole purpose of finding religion is a means to convince the authorities to grant them an early release. The difference with Berkowitz, however, is that he understands that he will most likely never be released from prison, yet after thirty-four years of preaching the word of

God, his stance has been unrelenting. Where a gimmick would begin to falter at the lack of a promise of release, Berkowitz has done the opposite of this, his faith and belief in positivity has only gained in momentum. It would be extremely difficult to maintain such a stance should it be nothing more than a gimmick.

Should the penalty for Capital crimes have been different in New York at the time of Berkowitz's sentencing, where life imprisonment was exchanged for the penalty of death, then the world would have missed out on the transformation of the Son of Sam. Berkowitz himself recognises that his life at the time of the murders, as well as the murders themselves, were shrouded in nothing short of an evil grasp. Yet, owing to the fact that the maximum sentence that was able to be given to him was the multiple life sentences, it has provided the opportunity for Berkowitz to become the shining example of how some Serial Killers are able to turn their lives around. It is arguable that given his missionary work for the church, Berkowitz has ultimately saved more lives than he has taken.

The pathway that Berkowitz was on during the 1970's could easily be likened to that of the destruction of an oncoming train. Yet, Berkowitz was able to steer clear of this destruction and lead almost three and a half decades of a pathway becoming a shining light. It does not take away the despair that was caused by his actions during the Son of Sam murders, however, his example to others may have saved many a life in the time beyond that.

An aspect of Berkowitz's transformation away from the mindset that was seemingly beyond repair in the views of the experts, is that Berkowitz feels as though God is with him, regardless of his physical surroundings. What remains to be seen is whether or not Berkowitz will be gifted the opportunity to avail of his positive work outside of the prison walls, should he ever be released. An example of this would be Michael Franzese, who was jailed for ten years on mafia related charges, only to spend decades following his release preaching the word of God as well as being a motivational speaker with positive results. Something he continues to do to this day.

Granted that racketeering crimes in relation to the Mafia are not in the same category as serial murder, however, should there ever be a candidate in which to be given the opportunity in which to prove the same levels of a positive transformation, then surely the ideal person would be, the world of serial murder's shining light, the Son of Hope, a one David Berkowitz?

If ever there was a case which contrasts the diagnosis of experts in relation to the mental state or potential of a Serial Killer, then the case for Berkowitz is the prime example. The evidence of the signs of remorse in Berkowitz are clearly evident to see. As well as his words being reinforced by the continual actions which he continues to display. Berkowitz is proof that there really can be a case made for empathy in death.

<u>Conclusion</u>

<u>When Black and White is read.</u>

The world of the Serial Killer is clearly not one that can be defined as simply black and white. There are as many variables in the types of killers that constantly emerge as there are victims in which they prey upon.

The variants that emerge within the world of murder evolve as much as the times in which we live in. With each aspect of current affairs, media outlets, as well as social circumstances constantly changing, so does the way that we view the world. Therefore, the aspects which drive a person to commit crimes is just as ever changing. Therefore, a suitable approach to the way we view murder should be as interchangeable and adaptable.

Each person who has devolved to serial murder has had their own attributes which has served as a trigger to their devolution. In the 1970's we had David Berkowitz and Ted Bundy, in the 80's we have Gary Ridgeway and the likes of Richard Ramirez, as well as a new type of Serial Killer in where even the less likely female gender were compelled to commit murder, such as Aileen Wuornos. In the 1990's we became aware of high-profile members of the public, such as Dr Harold Shipman in the United Kingdom, had devolved to murder.

The point is that, although each of these examples given are all guilty of the crime of serial murder, each of the examples were compelled to kill by entirely different reasons. Therefore, as the crime of serial murder has (de)evolved, therefore, the approach in which we have entrusted psychiatrists to diagnosis the murderers also have a requirement to evolve as well. Trying to place each of these Serial Killers into an already existing "box" for diagnosis does not seem accurate in an ever-evolving time.

It is acceptable to understand that a certain diagnosis may fit one of these killers in that certain aspects of their diagnosis may fit perfectly, but that does not mean that they all shall. With the identification of traits such as emotion, compartmentalisation, or even a neurological disorder giving rise to the theory that behaviour is often subject to change, then an accompanying theory is that the emotional aspects of the killer are potentially open to the same amount of possible change as well. Meaning that, like all aspects of evolutional change, the mindset of the Serial Killer has the potential to the same natural cycles.

Psychiatrists deserve respect for the years of dedication that they devote to their studies while obtaining their qualifications, however, there is an argument that instead of being rigid in a psychological belief system, there should a system in where there is the equal transformation of a diagnosis technique to model against the ever-changing mannerisms of the Serial Killer. Psychological profilers for police institutes such as the F.B.I for example, are constantly developing their approach in terms of psychology so that they can combine these studies in coalition with police detection so that they can not only catch Serial Killers at the earliest stage possible, but also in an attempt at preventing the opportunities for new Serial Killers to emerge. Thanks to people such as Robert D Keppel, in where an educated approach to combining all of these aspects of Serial Killer detection has created a pathway for other criminal profilers to follow.

The purpose of this book has been to shed a plausibility of a new light to be shone on the mindset and emotional aspects of serial murder. It is not to remove the theories and diagnosis that have been in place for years, but instead to build and expand on current belief systems. Giving rise that nothing in terms of psychology is ever black and white or concrete, but there is a clear and evident potential for further sub categories which are more adaptable to fit adequately to alternate diagnoses.

There are some Serial Killers, Mass Murderers, or even Career Criminals who will never have the mental capacity to be able to feel or understand the emotion of remorse. Even with some of the examples that I have provided, some of the perpetrators can be said to have not felt any forms of remorse at the time of their killing sprees. However, just as the example of neurological repair has been present within people who have suffered strokes or diseases such as dementia, it is just as plausible that a neurological repair scenario is possible in the case for Serial Killers. This gives suggestion that the possibility for remorse is just as plausible in these instances.

Although the two cases are not alike in nature, both Ted Bundy and David Berkowitz gave accounts of genuine remorse for their victims, however, the contrasting factor is that Bundy was put to death, whereas Berkowitz continues to give avenues for positive development with his work in the name of the church. Even with that, a person of Bundy's nature would never have been deemed a suitable candidate for release from prison, whereas Berkowitz could arguably be seen as a prime example to try such an experiment.

This gives all the more reason to suggest that no two Serial Killers are the same, therefore, should it not also be that no two Serial Killers should be given the same diagnosis? We are not limited by how we define things in life; therefore, we should not be limited to how we diagnose criminals, or even neurological disorders within criminals. The vast majority of books that we read, or even the television documentaries that we watch on the subject of true crime, is geared toward learning the mindset of the killer in question. Although we view these documentaries as a form of modern entertainment, with an expanding network on true crime programmes, we should be looking to be equally expanding our horizons in terms of each crime perpetrator as an individual, as opposed to a generalised collective.

In my research, I have corresponded with a multitude of Serial Killers, which have included writing to David Berkowitz, Gary Ridgeway, as well as speaking to other authors and psychologists. It has become apparent that there is no defining line when it comes to the mind of a Serial Killer, nor the potential for investigation into their individual mental state at various points in their respective timelines. Therefore, it would be remis to end the quest for knowledge at the base of an individual theory.

If anything, the reading of books on the subject, as well as watching expert testimony and opinion in documentaries raises as many questions as it does answers. As a result, this will only serve to spur on the desire for more knowledge and alternate viewpoints. The devolution of a Serial Killer has served as the birth for a need for an evolution of answers and new theories to accompany each case on an individual basis. It is a case of understanding the old so that we can research the new. In a world of true crime, it would be a crime in itself to rest on our laurels and come to the conclusion that we now know everything. Each day is a new dawn, with that comes new possibilities. However, we cannot even begin to discuss the events of a new day if we are clinging to aspects of the previous, all the while assuming that the two are exactly the same.

The End

<u>Authors Notes.</u>

The world of true crime has always been as much a fascination to me as is the world of horror and suspense in fiction. Although the two are not linked, they both provide an escape into a world of darkness beyond the realms of my own. It is by delving deep into these alternate worlds that I have come to truly appreciate my existence of positivity in my private life.

I am a person who does not take many things at face value, as I tend to be overtly inquisitive and wish to know all angles of a subject that I am interested in. After reading countless books and watching an equal amount of documentaries on the subject of serial murder, I began to ask myself questions as to the cold and sadistic approach that some of the serial killers tended to "display" in terms of the lives of their victims. I tried to understand how it came to fruition that a person could be deemed to be void of emotion, at not only the victims themselves, but also with regard to their lack of emotional states during sentencing, knowing that some of these killers would never see the light of day again.

It made me question the lack of remorse, guilt, and even apathy. I began to see through some of the cracks in the way that these cases were presented, which served only to make me delve further into the subject as a whole. The result of this is my latest foray, which you have just read. The sub categories of true crime are as deep as any other forms of non-fiction; therefore, you can rest assured that my journey into this world does not end here. There will certainly be more works from me on these subjects.

I have a great deal to be thankful for. For one, I have a wonderful partner in Kelly, who not only puts up with my ideas and endless research into the subjects that I delve into but is also fully supportive of everything that I do. Without her, I would not be in such a fortunate position where I am able to write about what captures my interest. Therefore, as always, my heart and soul give her endless thanks. I am extremely grateful, and I love you with all of my being.

I would also like to thank each and every one of you who read my books. You allow me to pursue my dream of writing. I only hope that I can continue to offer you the quality of content which matches your wonderful support.

I appreciate that a book based on the antics of various serial killings may not be the place to be dishing out heartfelt messages, however, there are people who I could not leave out in terms of acknowledgement. My Sister Charlene and her husband Rob. Our wee one Saya, who whilst approaching those torrid teenage years, continues to remain in awe of what I have accomplished. My writing companions, Ben, Brucetopher, Lilith and the now sadly departed Lucy-fur (furries) who never leave my side, although I am convinced that it is because I am the holder of cat treats. My family and friends, Eileen, Michelle, and all at Valhalla.

Additional thanks go to Sondra London, David Berkowitz and his representatives, as well as other persons who I have been in contact with in terms of research.

As always, my wonderful but sadly departed Mother Lynda, who I maintain that I would not have started writing were it not for the years of sharing books and stories with. I miss you each and every day.

I love you all with everything that I have.
Remember, the only darkness that exists is
the one in your imagination.

B.K Jackson.